TEA PARTY BIBLE TIMES FOR Mom and Me

MARY J. MURRAY

HARVEST HOUSE PUBLISHERS
EUGENE, OREGON

Cover illustration © Stockxpert / Jupiterimages Unlimited

Cover by Koechel Peterson & Associates, Inc., Minneapolis, Minnesota

Safety Alert

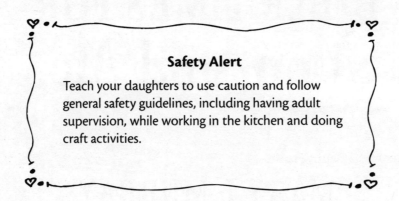

Teach your daughters to use caution and follow general safety guidelines, including having adult supervision, while working in the kitchen and doing craft activities.

TEA PARTY BIBLE TIMES FOR MOM AND ME

Published by Harvest House Publishers
Eugene, Oregon 97402
www.harvesthousepublishers.com

ISBN 978-0-7369-2862-5

Printed in the United States of America

10 11 12 13 14 15 16 17 18 / VP-KB / 10 9 8 7 6 5 4 3 2 1

Contents

Creating Wonderful Mother–Daughter Times

The mother–daughter relationship is a precious gift from God. This special bond you have with your daughter is a treasure to be cherished and nurtured. *Tea Party Bible Times for Mom and Me* will help you establish a loving relationship with your daughter, enhance your communication, and build trust between the two of you as you get together on a regular basis to share your thoughts, read Scripture, pray, and spend time together having fun and fellowship.

Tea Party Bible Times for Mom and Me is designed for you—a busy mom. All you need is approximately 30 minutes a day to complete one lesson each week. We'll cover eight topics that are important in the lives of girls: inner beauty, how we use our words, being content, kindness, friendship, money, family and home, and knowing God. Each chapter also includes unique tea party ideas, along with many extra opportunities for you and your daughter to enjoy as you work together in the kitchen, get creative, and share your time and thoughts.

The arts and craft projects provided within each chapter reinforce the study topic and make learning God's Word fun and meaningful for your daughter. The journal activities will enhance your relationship as you and your daughter reflect on your lives and share what you've been learning.

At the back of the book you'll find a "Mom and Me" decorative stationery page. Please feel free to make copies and use it for the writing projects in this book. You and your daughter might also enjoy using this special page for letters to family and friends.

Upon completion of this book, be sure to put it in a special place. You'll want it for a keepsake so you can enjoy looking through it in the years to come. It will be a great way to rekindle cherished memories and to measure the growth that has taken place in your lives and in your relationship with each other.

Tea Party Bible Times for Mom and Me is ideal for group Bible studies as well. Invite some other mother–daughter pairs to meet with you on a weekly basis. Complete a lesson together at home, and then gather together to talk about what you've learned as you go through the pages of the chapter in a group setting. You'll develop and enhance friendships that are grounded in the Word of God.

My prayer is that this book will help you and your daughter develop a relationship firmly established in the Word of God as you work toward becoming more like Him together.

"May the God of hope fill you with all joy and peace as you trust in him, so that you may overflow with hope by the power of the Holy Spirit" (Romans 15:13).

If you and your daughter enjoy this book, you'll have fun going through Mary's book *Just Mom and Me Having Tea.*

Sincerely,

Mary Murray

Getting Ready for a Tea Party

There are eight tea party celebrations in this book. Each one has a special theme and includes many unique ideas to make your time together memorable. You can create a tea party that is as simple or as elaborate as you like by trying some or all of the extra fun activities listed. Pick and choose what works best for you and your daughter.

Have fun together as you gather these basic tea party supplies to be used at each celebration:

- selection of tea bags
- teapot
- cups, saucers, spoons
- cream and sugar
- colorful place mats
- colorful napkins
- table decorations (see chapter suggestions)

There are many varieties and flavors of tea for you to enjoy at your tea parties. Girls may prefer sweeter flavored teas such as apple cinnamon, orange spice, strawberry, or mixed berry. And you don't have to drink hot tea. Hot cocoa, lemonade, fruit juice, lemon water, chocolate milk, and flavored ice tea are great alternatives.

Planning Ahead

Read through the "Having Fun Together" and Tea Party Celebration sections of each chapter several days before you'll be meeting so you can pick up the materials, supplies, and ingredients you'll need. Having the supplies on hand will make your time together more enjoyable.

Most of the materials and art supplies required for activities are common items that can be found within the home. Here is a short list of inexpensive supplies you may want to pick up at a craft store, department store, or rummage sale in case you want to try some of the extra fun activities mentioned in each chapter:

- artificial flowers
- balloons
- chenille sticks/pipe cleaners
- clay pot
- colored felt
- colored tissue paper
- craft foam
- craft wire
- decoupage or Modge Podge
- embroidery floss and large-eye sewing needles
- fabric paints or paint pens
- fabric scraps
- glue gun and glue sticks
- "peel and stick" magnets
- sequins, jewels, beads
- watercolor paints and paper
- white and colored card stock
- yarn and crochet hooks or knitting needles

For extra fun, use colored pencils to color the mothers, daughters, and other illustrations in this book.

Creating Fancy Lettering

Use "fancy lettering" to make your projects in this book look even more special. Here are quick and easy ways to create fancy letters. Print the words in your usual handwriting. Then add a curl, a dot, a circle, a bar, or a line at the ends and corners of each letter like the ones shown here. Use different color pens or markers if you like.

curl dot circle line bar

You can also add detail to your letters with a row of fun dots on all the rounded letters:

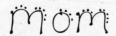

mom

stitches near the straight lines:

or swirls inside closed letters:

Try adding small hearts, stars, dots, and flowers to make your words look even more creative and fun.

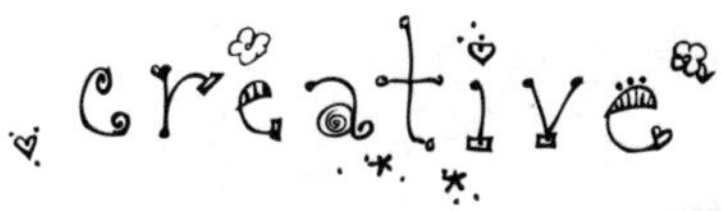

Now try some fancy lettering of your own!

Drawing Fun Girls and Women

You'll probably want to draw pictures of your mom and you in several of the activities found in this book. If you're unsure how to draw people, here are some quick and easy steps to help you. Use the space on the right side to practice the drawing steps. Have fun adding details as you create hairstyles, clothing, and accessories, such as barrettes, hair bands, flowers, hearts, jewelry, hats, glasses.

1. Draw the ears and chin using one smooth stroke.

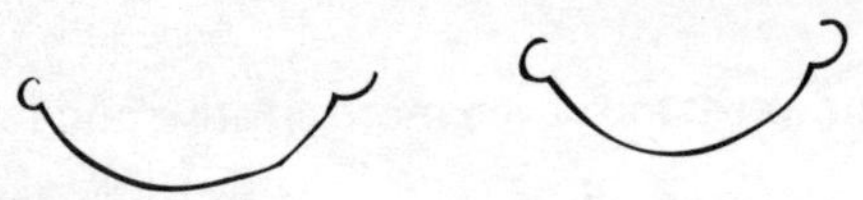

2. Add a face and neck.

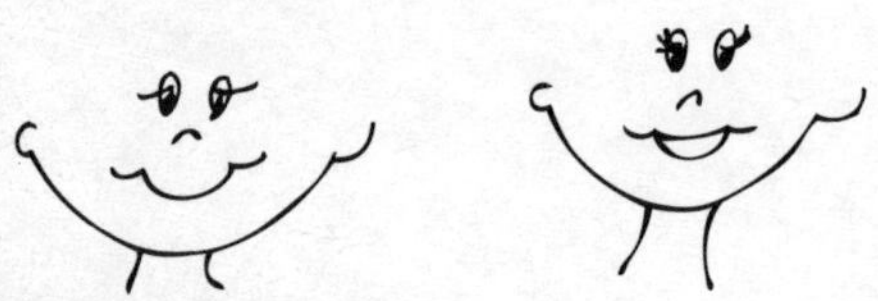

3. Add hair, fun and colorful clothing, and other details.

Mom and Me

Chapter 1

Beautiful on the Inside

The LORD does not look at the things man looks at. Man looks at the outward appearance, but the LORD looks at the heart.

1 SAMUEL 16:7

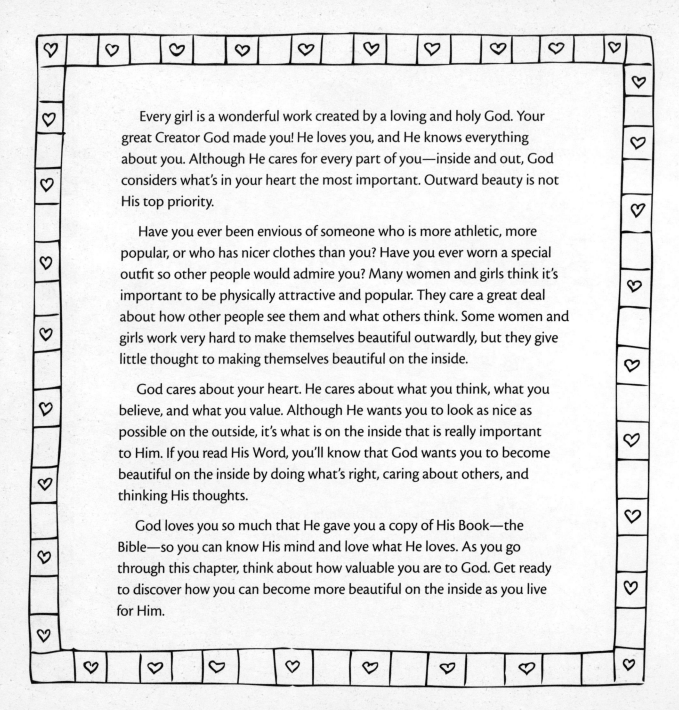

Every girl is a wonderful work created by a loving and holy God. Your great Creator God made you! He loves you, and He knows everything about you. Although He cares for every part of you—inside and out, God considers what's in your heart the most important. Outward beauty is not His top priority.

Have you ever been envious of someone who is more athletic, more popular, or who has nicer clothes than you? Have you ever worn a special outfit so other people would admire you? Many women and girls think it's important to be physically attractive and popular. They care a great deal about how other people see them and what others think. Some women and girls work very hard to make themselves beautiful outwardly, but they give little thought to making themselves beautiful on the inside.

God cares about your heart. He cares about what you think, what you believe, and what you value. Although He wants you to look as nice as possible on the outside, it's what is on the inside that is really important to Him. If you read His Word, you'll know that God wants you to become beautiful on the inside by doing what's right, caring about others, and thinking His thoughts.

God loves you so much that He gave you a copy of His Book—the Bible—so you can know His mind and love what He loves. As you go through this chapter, think about how valuable you are to God. Get ready to discover how you can become more beautiful on the inside as you live for Him.

The Bible Says...

I praise you because I am fearfully and wonderfully made; your works are wonderful, I know that full well.

PSALM 139:14

Think about this verse as you work through the lesson.

Memorize It!

See who can be the first to memorize this verse.
Once you have it in your heart, check it off.

Mom ☐

Me ☐

Sharing Our Thoughts

Make my joy complete by being like-minded, having the same love, being one in spirit and purpose.

PHILIPPIANS 2:2

Talk about these questions and ideas together. Write down some of your thoughts in the spaces provided.

1. What are some things women and girls do to make themselves attractive to others?

2. How do television, movies, and magazines portray girls and women?

3. Share about someone you know who looks good outwardly, but who isn't very nice on the inside.

4. In what ways can you model inner beauty—a beautiful heart or spirit that is pleasing to God?

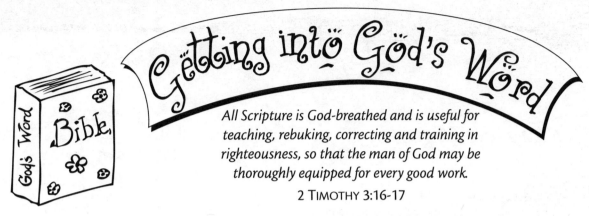

Getting into God's Word

All Scripture is God-breathed and is useful for teaching, rebuking, correcting and training in righteousness, so that the man of God may be thoroughly equipped for every good work.

2 TIMOTHY 3:16-17

Open your Bibles to 1 Peter 3:3-6. In this passage, Peter explains how women and girls who believe in God and Jesus should live. He tells women they can please God by having an inner beauty that is gentle, quiet, submissive; by doing what's right; and by not fearing anything. Peter reminds women to be like Sarah, not focusing on outward beauty, but working on their inner beauty that is of great worth in God's sight.

You will be blessed by God as you put this into practice today. Read 1 Peter 3:3-6 aloud together. Talk about ways you can develop that special inner beauty—the beautiful heart that God loves.

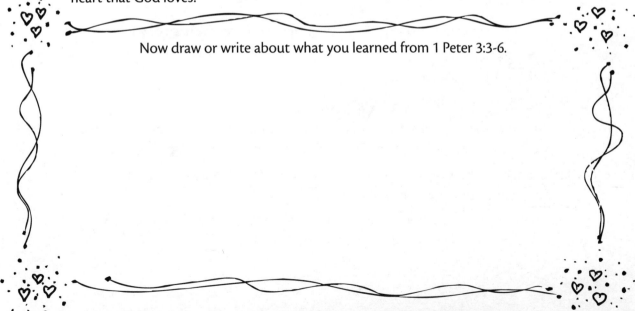

Now draw or write about what you learned from 1 Peter 3:3-6.

Having Fun Together

Decorative Mirror

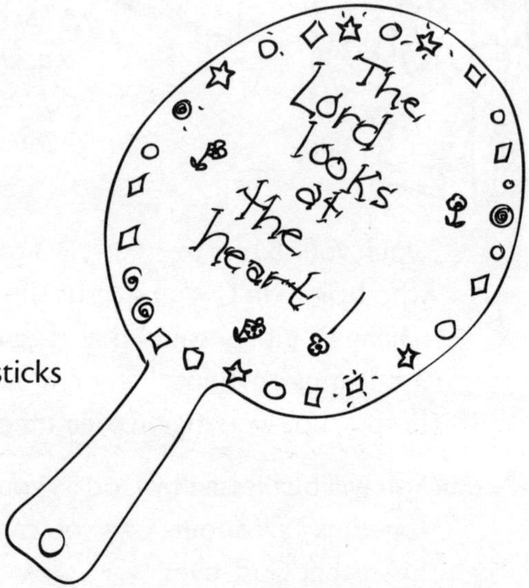

Here's What You Need

- pocket or hand-held mirror
- colored construction paper
- fine-line black marking pen
- glue, glue stick, or cool melt glue gun with glue sticks
- markers or colored pencils
- *Optional:* sequins, jewels, beads

Here's What to Do

1. Cut a piece of colored construction paper that will fit on the back of your mirror.
2. Using the black marker and your fanciest handwriting, write on it: "The LORD looks at the heart!" (1 Samuel 16:7).
3. Glue the paper securely to the mirror.
4. Using the glue, add a border of sequins, jewels, and/or beads to the edge of the paper, making a frame around the Scripture verse. Let it dry overnight.
5. Each time you use the mirror to look at your outward beauty, remember to think about your inner beauty and how to please God.
6. Show the mirror to a friend or family member, and tell him or her what you've learned about making yourself beautiful on the inside.

Just God and Me

Be transformed by the renewing of your mind.
Then you will be able to test and approve what God's
will is—his good, pleasing and perfect will.

ROMANS 12:2

Look up these Scripture passages during the week to help you think like God does regarding beauty.

Day of the Week	Verse	Something to Think About
Monday	Matthew 6:25-33	How do these verses help you to think about your clothing and your outward appearance?
Tuesday	1 Samuel 16:7	When the Lord looks at your heart, what does He see?
Wednesday	1 Timothy 2:9-10	What do these verses say about how women and girls should dress and how they should spend their time?
Thursday	Romans 12:2	Think about the patterns of this world regarding outward beauty. What is God's will for you in becoming a beautiful person?
Friday	Isaiah 52:7	What does this verse say about beauty? What good news of salvation can you share with others?
Saturday	Proverbs 3:5-7	How can you stop being "wise in your own eyes" and acknowledge God's ways regarding inner beauty and outward beauty?
Sunday	Psalm 100	What are some of the ways you can please the Lord, thank the Lord, and praise the Lord?

Talking to God

Devote yourselves to prayer, being watchful and thankful.
COLOSSIANS 4:2

Dear God,
Thank You so much for creating me perfectly and for caring about every detail of my life. Help me become more pleasing in Your sight. I want to think like You think and love what You love. Help me concentrate less on my outward beauty and focus more on my inner beauty because that is what's most important to You. Let the words of Peter rest in my heart as I develop a spirit that is quiet, gentle, submissive, and not afraid. In Jesus' name I pray. Amen.

Pray this prayer or write your own prayer thanking God for creating you. Ask Him to help you think His thoughts about beauty.

Things to Pray About

Think of one thing each of you needs prayer for. Write them down in the space provided. Talk about them together, and remember to pray for each other this week.

Daughter

Mom

Do not be anxious about anything, but in everything, by prayer and petition, with thanksgiving, present your requests to God.
PHILIPPIANS 4:6

Proverbs 31 for Girls

The Proverbs 31 girl knows outward beauty lasts a short time but inner beauty pleases God and has everlasting value.

Charm is deceptive, and beauty is fleeting;
but a woman who fears the LORD is to be praised.

PROVERBS 31:30

After reading Proverbs 31:30, think about what you can do to become more like the woman in Proverbs 31.

My Plan

1.

2.

3.

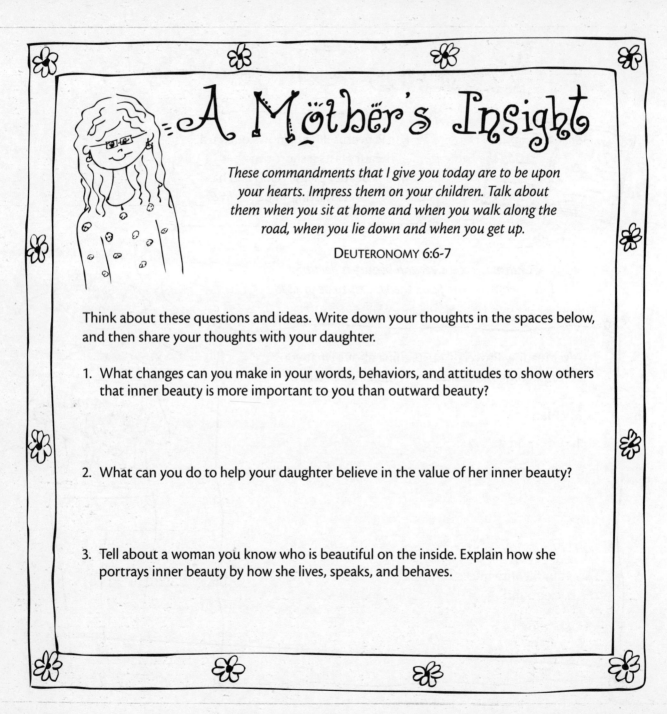

A Mother's Insight

These commandments that I give you today are to be upon your hearts. Impress them on your children. Talk about them when you sit at home and when you walk along the road, when you lie down and when you get up.

DEUTERONOMY 6:6-7

Think about these questions and ideas. Write down your thoughts in the spaces below, and then share your thoughts with your daughter.

1. What changes can you make in your words, behaviors, and attitudes to show others that inner beauty is more important to you than outward beauty?

2. What can you do to help your daughter believe in the value of her inner beauty?

3. Tell about a woman you know who is beautiful on the inside. Explain how she portrays inner beauty by how she lives, speaks, and behaves.

A Formal Tea Party

Whatever you do, whether in word or deed, do it all in the name of the Lord Jesus, giving thanks to God the Father through him.

COLOSSIANS 3:17

Creating a Fabulous Tea Party Setting

Along with the party supplies and suggestions in the introduction, try some of these special touches:

- Display a photo of the two of you in the center of the table. You can also include photos of the two of you at various life stages.
- Put on your dressiest clothes, fancy hats, and elegant gloves. (Thrift stores often have old-fashioned hats and gloves.)
- Cut out an assortment of heart shapes from colored construction paper. Write "Mom," "Me," or "God" on each heart. Sprinkle the hearts randomly on the table as a reminder of your love for each other and for God.
- Place a colorful bouquet of flowers in the center of the table.
- On a large sheet of card stock write and display this phrase: "Mothers and daughters make the world a beautiful place to be."
- Light two candles and place them on the table.
- Play your favorite music softly in the background.

Tea Party Psalm

Read Psalm 139:1-18 aloud together and talk about how God lovingly created you.

Having Fun Together

Make colorful paper beads. Wrap 1 x 8-inch strips of colored paper tightly around a pencil. Apply transparent tape. Write "Mom and Me!" or "Mom," "Me," and "And" on each bead and slide off pencil. String beads together and attach them to your backpack, purse, or bedroom mirror.

Two beautiful hearts. Cut two 8-inch hearts from card stock or cardboard. Use art supplies and collage materials to decorate the hearts. Be creative and have fun! Give the heart to the other person "for keeps" to remind her of your love.

Scrapbook page or poster. Have someone take a photo of the two of you as you enjoy your tea. Glue the photo to the scrapbook page or to a piece of cardboard, title it "Mom and Me" and decorate with words, stickers, and drawings.

Playful T-shirts. Using colorful fabric paints, write "Mom and Me!" on white T-shirts. Then draw fun pictures of yourselves and add bright details. After the shirts are dry, put them on and share with your family how much you enjoyed your tea party.

"Mom and Me" necklace. Use 2 bread twist ties or 2 pieces of bendable wire for each "person" you make. Take one twist tie and form the legs and torso. With the other twist tie form arms and a loop for the head. Connect the two pieces together with one of the ends of the twist ties. Wrap strands of embroidery floss through the head loop for hair. Wrap colorful embroidery floss around the body for clothes. String the "mother" and "daughter" together to create a necklace.

More Fun Ideas

"I love you" letters. Copy stationery page (end of book) and write a love note to the other person. Place it in an envelope and tuck it under the other person's pillow.

Encourage one another. Take turns completing the following sentences for each other:

- Mom, you have a beautiful heart because…
- Daughter, you have a beautiful heart because…

Say thank you. Write a letter to God thanking Him for creating you just as you are. Be specific about your God-given talents, gifts, strengths, and even weaknesses.

No fear! First Peter 3:6 says to "do what is right and do not give way to fear." Write things you sometimes fear on slips of paper (one per paper). Crumple up the papers, and take turns tossing them one-by-one into a trash can as you choose to trust God instead of being afraid.

Photo fun. Use a bold marker and write on a sheet of paper: "I'm beautiful inside and out!" Take photos of each other in various poses while holding the sign. Set up the pictures as a slide show on your computer as a reminder that God created you beautifully.

Menu Suggestions

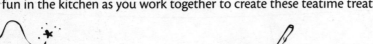

Have fun in the kitchen as you work together to create these teatime treats!

Fruit Fizzle Punch

Ingredients

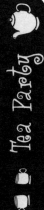

ice cubes
1/2 cup orange juice, chilled
1/2 cup cranberry juice or fruit juice, chilled
pineapple juice (from a can of pineapple), chilled
1 can clear soda pop, regular or sugar-free
2 toothpicks
6 medium chunks of pineapple
2 slices of orange
2 straws

Directions

1. Place ice cubes in two tall glasses. Pour the chilled fruit juices over the ice.
2. Slowly add the clear soda pop and watch it bubble and fizz.
3. Skewer three pineapple chunks onto each toothpick and drop one into each glass.
4. Use a knife to make a slit in each orange slice. Slide the slice over the lip of the glass for decoration.
5. Insert a straw and enjoy.

Stackable Snackables

Ingredients

thin slices of cheese
thin slices of turkey, ham, or sausage
olives, cut in half
assorted snack crackers
cream cheese or cheese spread

Directions

1. Cut the cheese and meats into one-inch square slices.
2. On a cracker, place a slice of meat, a slice of cheese, the cheese spread, and top with an olive.
3. Be creative and come up with your own combinations!

Cookie Ice Cream Sandwiches

Ingredients

vanilla or chocolate ice cream
four chocolate chip cookies

Directions

1. Allow the ice cream to soften in the refrigerator for 20 minutes.
2. Spread a small scoop of ice cream on two cookies.
3. Top with another cookie and press together.
4. Wrap the ice cream cookies in plastic and store them in freezer for two hours minimum to harden the ice cream.
5. Take out and enjoy.

Chapter 2

Words Are Important

Let the word of Christ dwell in you richly as you teach and admonish one another with all wisdom, and as you sing psalms, hymns and spiritual songs with gratitude in your hearts to God.

COLOSSIANS 3:16

Have you ever spoken something out loud and then later wished you hadn't? The words you speak are very important. What you say tells a lot about what you believe and what you value. Your words show people what is in your heart and what kind of a person you are. Hopefully your words let people know you are a thankful, thoughtful, kind, and caring person.

You can use your words to share your thoughts and ideas, help others get to know you better, and talk with others about your Lord and Savior, Jesus Christ. You can also use your words to help people grow and change so they can please God even more.

Some girls don't think before they speak, and their words end up hurting other people. Some girls talk too much, talk too loudly, or talk when they aren't supposed to. Have you ever spoken quickly without thinking how your words will sound? Sometimes you might talk in a way that causes people to think being a Christian is bad, especially when you're angry, complaining, speaking impatiently, arguing, or gossiping. You can disappoint God if your words don't line up with what He says in His Book to us—the Bible.

God wants you to be very careful with what you say. He wants you to be an example to others by how you live and how you speak. What you say matters a lot! Do you need to make any changes in how you speak? What can you say so your words will please God and benefit other people?

The Bible Says...

May the words of my mouth and the meditation of my heart be pleasing in your sight, O LORD*, my Rock and my Redeemer.*

PSALM 19:14

Think about this verse as you work through the lesson.

Memorize It!

See who can be the first to memorize this verse.
Once you have it in your heart, check it off.

Mom ☐

Me ☐

Sharing Our Thoughts

Make my joy complete by being like-minded, having the same love, being one in spirit and purpose.

PHILIPPIANS 2:2

Talk about these questions and ideas together. Write down some of your thoughts in the spaces provided.

1. How can you use your words to encourage the people in your family?

2. What can you say to people about your great God?

3. Share about a time when your words helped another person. And then tell about a time when your words hurt someone.

4. Tell about a time when another person's words encouraged and helped you.

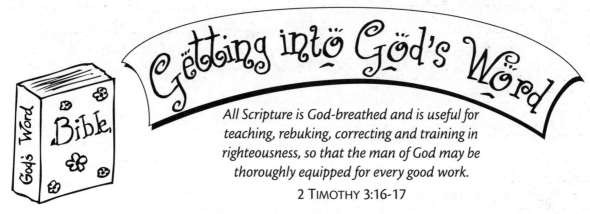

Getting into God's Word

All Scripture is God-breathed and is useful for teaching, rebuking, correcting and training in righteousness, so that the man of God may be thoroughly equipped for every good work.

2 TIMOTHY 3:16-17

Open your Bibles to James 3:8-12. In this passage, James notes that people speak words of praise to God and speak words that curse people. God doesn't want us to be like that. He wants only goodness to come from our mouths and hearts.

Think about the words that come from your heart and mouth. Would any of them displease God? If yes, make the decision to put an end to saying things that aren't pleasing to Him.

Read James 3:8-12 aloud together. Talk about how you can use your words to please God.

Now draw or write about what you learned from James 3:8-12.

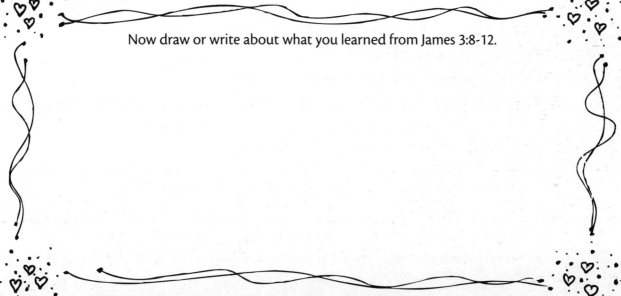

Having Fun Together

Cheerful Candleholder

Here's What You Need

- ✩ glass jar, clean and dry
- ✩ 3 or more colors of tissue paper
- ✩ ¼ cup of water in shallow bowl or cup
- ✩ scissors
- ✩ 1 tablespoon glue (liquid)
- ✩ paintbrush
- ✩ permanent black marker or black paint marker
- ✩ tea light or votive candle

Here's What to Do

1. Cut ten or more one-inch squares from each color of tissue paper.
2. Place ¼ cup of water in a bowl.
3. Add a drizzle (about 1 tablespoon) of glue, and then stir.
4. Paint a portion of the jar with the glue solution. Then lay several tissue squares on the sticky jar, overlapping one another. Paint over the tissue squares with more solution. Continue until the jar is covered. Let dry overnight.
5. Use a black marker and your fancy handwriting to write encouraging phrases on the jar, such as "I love God," "I can help," "I'm thankful," and "God is great."
6. Place a tea light candle or plastic tea light inside the candleholder and display it on the kitchen table. This candle will remind you to be a light to people when you speak. Light the candle at your next meal and share what you've learned about the importance of words.

Just God and Me

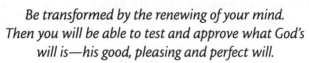

Be transformed by the renewing of your mind.
Then you will be able to test and approve what God's
will is—his good, pleasing and perfect will.

ROMANS 12:2

Look up these Scripture passages during the week to help you learn more about using words that please God.

Day of the Week	Verse	Something to Think About
Monday	James 1:19	What does this verse say about how you should talk with and listen to others?
Tuesday	Acts 11:20-21	What might happen when you tell others the good news about believing in Jesus Christ as Savior and Lord?
Wednesday	Philippians 2:14-15	How can you be an example to others and speak in ways that please God?
Thursday	Ephesians 4:29	How can your words benefit people?
Friday	Proverbs 12:18	What might happen if you don't think before you speak? How can you help others by choosing your words carefully?
Saturday	Psalm 63	Like the psalmist, think of several things you can praise God for...and then do it!
Sunday	Ephesians 5:19-20	What do these verses say about how you should speak?

Talking to God

Devote yourselves to prayer, being watchful and thankful.
COLOSSIANS 4:2

Pray this prayer or write your own prayer praising God and asking Him to help you use your words wisely.

Dear God,
Thank You for Your Book that teaches me about the importance of my words. You are holy and righteous. Help me do well in speaking words that praise You and bring You glory. I want to only use words that are truthful and thankful. Let me show love for others by encouraging them and helping them. I want to please You in all I say and do. I will look for opportunities to tell people about You and Your Son, Jesus Christ. In His name I pray. Amen.

Things to Pray About

Think of one thing each of you needs prayer for. Write them down in the space provided. Talk about them together, and remember to pray for each other this week.

Daughter

Mom

Do not be anxious about anything, but in everything, by prayer and petition, with thanksgiving, present your requests to God.
PHILIPPIANS 4:6

Proverbs 31 for Girls

The Proverbs 31 girl is wise and faithful to God when she speaks.

She speaks with wisdom, and faithful instruction is on her tongue.
PROVERBS 31:26

After reading Proverbs 31:26, think about what you can do to become more like the woman in Proverbs 31.

My Plan

1.

2.

3.

A Daughter's Reflection

Teach me to do your will, for you are my God; may your good Spirit lead me on level ground.

Psalm 143:10

Think about these questions and ideas. Write down your thoughts in the spaces provided, and then share your thoughts with your mom.

1. Write down a specific compliment you can share with a family member or friend, and then be sure to do it.

2. What can you do to be a better example to others in how you speak?

3. If someone asked you what you know about Jesus Christ, what would you say?

4. What are some things you can say to show others that you love God?

A Slumber Tea Party

Whatever you do, whether in word or deed, do it all in the name of the Lord Jesus, giving thanks to God the Father through him.

COLOSSIANS 3:17

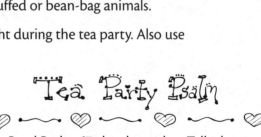

Creating a Fabulous Tea Party Setting

Along with the party supplies and suggestions in the introduction, try some of these special touches:

- Put on your favorite pajamas and warm slippers.
- Hold this party in the evening and turn down the lights for a cozy atmosphere.
- String Christmas lights about the area for extra sparkle.
- Light one or two candles and display them in a safe place.
- Cover a table with black fabric or paper to represent the night sky. Cut out an assortment of bright yellow paper stars and display them randomly on the table.
- Create a nighttime tea party setting in your living room: Unroll two sleeping bags, gather a pile of pillows, and scatter some favorite stuffed or bean-bag animals.
- Get two flashlights or a lantern and use them for light during the tea party. Also use them for nighttime reading and the fun activities.
- Set up a makeshift tent for you or the stuffed animals to sleep in.

Tea Party Psalm

Read Psalm 67 aloud together. Talk about how you can praise God by rejoicing in His great blessings in your life.

Having Fun Together

Gentle mayhem. Have a pillow fight. Remember to be gentle.

Sock war. Each person gathers five pairs of soft, colorful socks. Roll each sock inside itself, forming 10 balls each. Sit on opposite sides of the room and lob sock balls across the room at one another. (When the rest of the family sees how much fun you're having, they'll want to join in!)

Fun feet. Remove your shoelaces from your favorite pair of tennis shoes. Use paint markers or fine-line permanent markers and write "Mom and Me" on each lace. Add other decorative drawings. Let the laces dry and then put back in the shoes. Wear the shoes often!

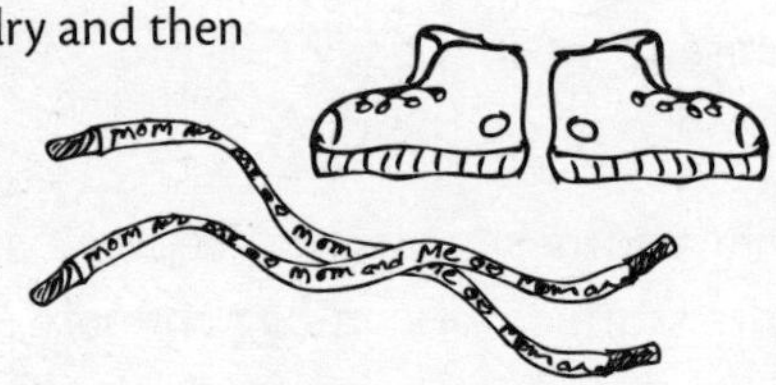

Word fun. Cut out an assortment of fun and encouraging words from magazines or newspapers. Using poster boards and glue, make collages for each other.

Stuffed pillows. Make personalized felt pillows. Cut four eight-inch squares from felt. Embroider your name onto one felt square. (There will be one square with "Mom" and one square with your name.) Attach a second piece of felt and sew the "pillow" together on three sides. Stuff the pillow with batting (quilt filler or old-but-clean socks or washcloths). Sew the last side closed. Display the pillows in the living room as a reminder of your fun time together.

More Fun Ideas

Puzzle fun. Create a word search or crossword puzzle using words and phrases that will please God. Exchange puzzles and see if you can solve them.

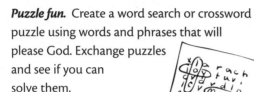

Number fun. Roll a die and then write or say an encouraging word using the specified number of letters. The other person will then use the word in a sentence that is pleasing to God.

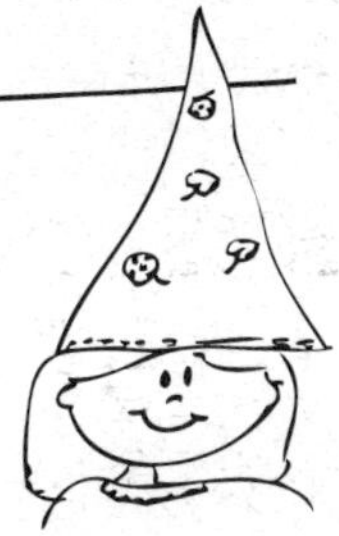

Make note cards. Make your own note cards using art and craft supplies. Write an encouraging message or favorite Scripture verse inside each card and then give them away during the week.

Create a game. Play a Scrabble-type word game by forming words that are good for people to hear. Make your own letter tiles for this activity by cutting card stock into one-inch squares and writing one consonant or vowel on each square. Make three squares for each consonant and six for each vowel.

Around and around. Write each other an encouraging, circular letter. Begin your first sentence in the center of a piece of drawing paper. Write the sentences in a circle, going around and around until you, finish your message. Then cut around your message, sign it, and give it to your tea party partner.

Menu Suggestions

Have fun in the kitchen as you work together to create these teatime treats!

Spiced Apple Cider Drink

Ingredients

apple cider or apple juice
nutmeg
cinnamon stick

Directions

1. Warm the cider in your microwave oven or on the stovetop. Pour into mugs.
2. Sprinkle a dash of nutmeg on top of the hot beverage and insert a cinnamon stick.
3. Let the cinnamon stick steep for two minutes and enjoy.

Mini Fruit Pizzas

Ingredients

rice cakes (or bagel halves or flour tortillas)
cream cheese, peanut butter, or jam
small pieces of fresh, dried, or canned fruits

Directions

1. Spread the cream cheese, peanut butter, or jam over each rice cake.
2. Top each "pizza" with small pieces of your favorite fruits and enjoy.

Indoor S'mores

Ingredients

graham crackers
mini marshmallows
chocolate, peanut butter, or butterscotch chips

Directions

1. Set two graham cracker halves on a microwave-safe plate.
2. Place five mini marshmallows on each cracker.
3. Place eight chocolate, peanut butter, or butterscotch chips on each cracker between the marshmallows.
4. Microwave for 10 seconds or until the marshmallows are puffed up.
5. Top with another cracker half, let cool slightly, and enjoy.

Mom and Me

Chapter 3

A Content and Happy Heart

Be joyful always; pray continually;
give thanks in all circumstances, for this is God's
will for you in Christ Jesus.

1 THESSALONIANS 5:16-18

God has been generous and good to you in many ways. He's given you a home, a family, friends, His Word, a church family, and much, much more. In His Book, God talks about how He wants you to be content and happy with what He's given you. He also says to be thankful and cheerful all the time. Even though God has been good to you, it can be easy to want more or to want something different. We all tend to be that way. You may sometimes wish you had different clothes, more friends, nicer belongings, or even a different brother or sister. You might even wish you looked different or that your parents would give you more privileges. Sometimes you may not be thankful for certain foods served for supper or events God has placed in your life to help you grow in Him.

Yes, the Bible says to be thankful at all times and to be content whether you have a lot or whether you have a little. Have you ever been around a person who wasn't thankful, wasn't content, and who complained a lot? Perhaps you have been that way at times. God doesn't want His people to live like that. You can develop a content and happy heart if you focus on how God has richly blessed you.

Let's explore how to put an end to unthankfulness and complaining and put on a "happy heart" for God. Remember, He loves you!

The Bible Says...

I have learned to be content
whatever the circumstances.

PHILIPPIANS 4:11

Think about this verse as you work through the lesson.

Memorize It!

See who can be the first to memorize this verse.
Once you have it in your heart, check it off.

Mom ☐

Me ☐

Sharing Our Thoughts

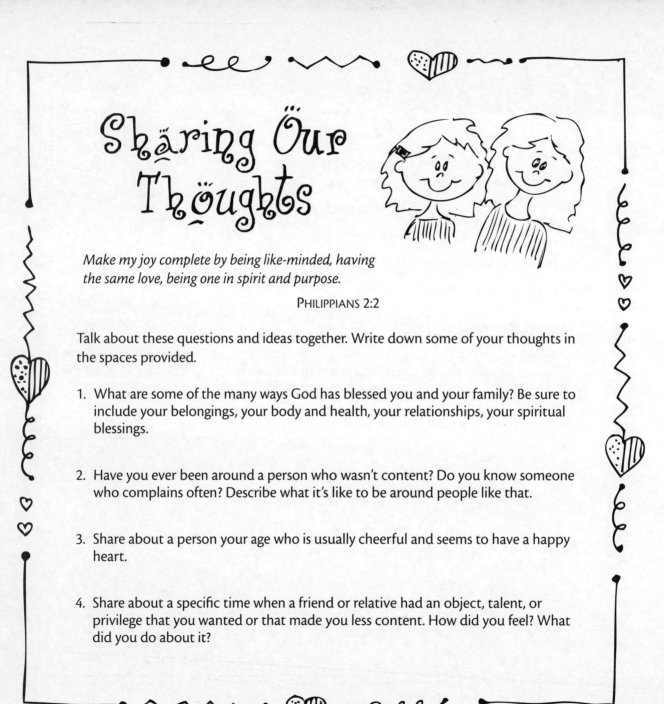

Make my joy complete by being like-minded, having the same love, being one in spirit and purpose.

PHILIPPIANS 2:2

Talk about these questions and ideas together. Write down some of your thoughts in the spaces provided.

1. What are some of the many ways God has blessed you and your family? Be sure to include your belongings, your body and health, your relationships, your spiritual blessings.

2. Have you ever been around a person who wasn't content? Do you know someone who complains often? Describe what it's like to be around people like that.

3. Share about a person your age who is usually cheerful and seems to have a happy heart.

4. Share about a specific time when a friend or relative had an object, talent, or privilege that you wanted or that made you less content. How did you feel? What did you do about it?

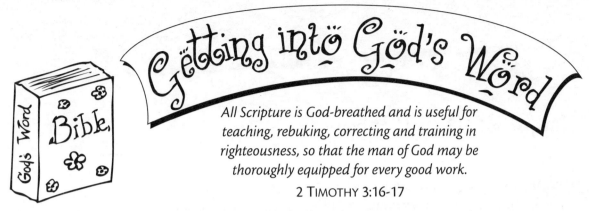

Getting into God's Word

All Scripture is God-breathed and is useful for teaching, rebuking, correcting and training in righteousness, so that the man of God may be thoroughly equipped for every good work.

2 TIMOTHY 3:16-17

Open your Bibles to Philippians 4:10-13. The Bible provides a lot of information about the apostle Paul. He became a follower of Jesus Christ after persecuting Christians. After becoming a Christian, Paul became a good example of what a content person acts like. He was imprisoned, mistreated, beat up, and suffered greatly because of his love for Jesus. Yet Paul continued to teach the importance of being content no matter what the circumstances are.

Read Philippians 4:10-13 aloud together. Talk about Paul's teaching on contentment and how you can become more content.

Now draw or write about what you learned from Philippians 4:10-13.

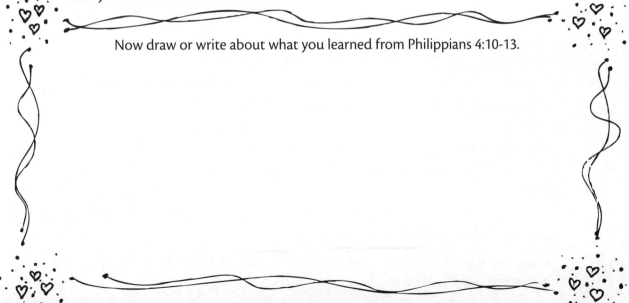

Having Fun Together

Happy Heart Puff Pillow

Here's What You Need

- ✩ 2 sheets (8½ x 11) colored copy paper, scrapbook paper, or wrapping paper
- ✩ scissors
- ✩ bold black marker
- ✩ facial tissue
- ✩ glue stick or needle and thread

Here's What to Do

1. Cut two large, identical heart shapes from the colored sheets of paper. If you hold the two pieces of paper together while you cut, the hearts will be exactly the same. If you're using wrapping paper, make sure the decorative side is facing out before you cut.
2. Using the marker and your fanciest lettering, write one of these phrases on the colored or decorative side of each heart: "Be content!" or "Have a Happy Heart!"
3. If using glue, rub a glue stick generously around the outer edge of one heart. Crumple one or two facial tissues and set them in the center of the heart with the glue on it. Place the second heart on top and press the edges together securely. You now have a puffy heart!
4. If using a needle and thread, sew the hearts together, leaving a small opening. Stuff the tissues inside and then close the opening.
5. Display your puffy pillow where you'll see it often and be reminded to have a content and happy heart for God.

Just God and Me

Be transformed by the renewing of your mind. Then you will be able to test and approve what God's will is—his good, pleasing and perfect will.

ROMANS 12:2

Look up these Scripture passages during the week to help you discover more about being content.

Day of the Week	Verse	Something to Think About
Monday	Philippians 2:14	Instead of complaining today, what can you say?
Tuesday	Habakkuk 3:17-18	How is Habakkuk a good example to you?
Wednesday	1 Timothy 6:8	How can you show that you are content with your food and clothing?
Thursday	Matthew 6:19-21	What do these verses teach about having a happy heart?
Friday	1 Thessalonians 5:16-18	Why is it important to rejoice, pray, and be thankful?
Saturday	Hebrews 13:5; Philippians 4:19	According to these verses, name two reasons why you should be content.
Sunday	James 1:2-8	How can these verses help you be joyful even when things aren't going the way you'd like?

Talking to God

Devote yourselves to prayer, being watchful and thankful.
Colossians 4:2

Dear God,
Thank You so much for being my God. Thank You for generously pouring out Your goodness in my life. I praise You for all You have given to me and all You have done. Help me, Lord, to become more content. Help me be thankful for my food, my home, my belongings, and every circumstance in my life. I want to be thankful for the way You created me. Help me be content with the people You've placed in my life. Thank You for Your great love and for Your abundant kindness to me. In Jesus' name I pray.
Amen.

Pray this prayer or write your own prayer thanking God for His kindness to you. Ask Him to help you become a content person who displays a happy heart.

Things to Pray About

Think of one thing each of you needs prayer for. Write them down in the space provided. Talk about them together, and remember to pray for each other this week.

Daughter

Mom

Do not be anxious about anything, but in everything, by prayer and petition, with thanksgiving, present your requests to God.
Philippians 4:6

Proverbs 31 for Girls

The Proverbs 31 girl is strong in God's truth. She looks forward to the days ahead without fear because she knows there is a place prepared for her in heaven with her Lord.

She is clothed with strength and dignity; she can laugh at the days to come.

PROVERBS 31:25

After reading Proverbs 31:25, think about what you can do to become more like the woman in Proverbs 31.

My Plan

1.

2.

3.

A Daughter's Reflection

Teach me to do your will, for you are my God; may your good Spirit lead me on level ground.

PSALM 143:10

Think about these questions and ideas. Write down your thoughts in the spaces provided, and then share your thoughts with your mom.

1. When are you most content?

2. Think of a place or situation (school, store, a friend's home) where you've been tempted to be unthankful and want something more or something different. Explain.

3. What can you do to be ready to counter those feelings and attitudes the next time they come?

4. List two or three things you can do to help yourself become a more content person.

Book Bonanza Tea Party

Whatever you do, whether in word or deed, do it all in the name of the Lord Jesus, giving thanks to God the Father through him.

COLOSSIANS 3:17

Creating a Fabulous Tea Party Setting

Along with the party supplies and suggestions in the Introduction, add some of these special touches:

- Create a cozy reading corner in your living room or bedroom, and host your Book Bonanza Tea Party there.
- Toss a few throw pillows or bean bag chairs on the floor, and set your tea and snacks on a nearby coffee table or serving tray.
- Cut several six-inch square shapes from colored construction paper. Fold each one in half to create a book shape. Sprinkle these about the table. During the tea, write the titles of your favorite books, books of Scripture, and Scripture verses on the book shapes.
- Have two reading lamps turned on, display a few stuffed animal friends, and two soft afghans or quilts to add a cozy touch to the Book Bonanza Tea Party.
- Display an assortment of your favorite books, magazines, and other reading material around the teatime area.
- Make a special sign that says "Book Bonanza." Decorate the sign using art supplies and display it on the teatime table.

Tea Party Psalm

Read Psalm 103 aloud together. Talk about God's goodness to you and all the reasons you have to praise Him.

Having Fun Together

Read aloud fun. Select a chapter from your favorite book. Read the chapter aloud while the other person listens and enjoys her tea and snacks.

Book talk. Choose a favorite book and give a "book talk." Tell the other person what you liked best about the book, describe a favorite character, and explain the plot and setting.

Surprise package. Visit a bookstore and purchase a book that you will both enjoy reading together. If the store offers free gift wrapping, have the book wrapped. At the Book Bonanza Tea Party, unwrap the book and set up a reading schedule so you each read a chapter from the book and then talk about it.

Chocolate chip blessings. Display 20 chocolate chips or other small edible items in the center of the table. As you sip your tea, take turns sharing one way God has blessed you. After each item, munch a chip. Continue until all chocolate chips have been eaten.

Write a book. Write your own story or create a book for children. Use colorful pens, pencils, paper, and art supplies to make it vibrant through fancy lettering and illustrations. Read the book to a young person in your family or neighborhood.

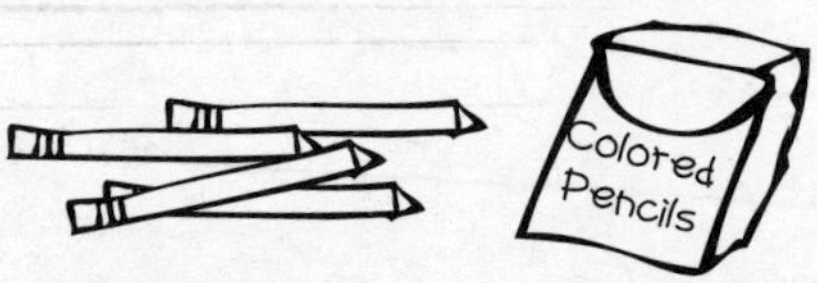

More Fun Ideas

A happy heart. Describe a person you know who has a "happy heart." For extra fun, use art supplies to create a colorful picture of this person.

Library visit. Take a trip to your local library and check out some books. Bring a treat and a thank-you card for the librarian to show your appreciation for the work he or she does in your community.

Box donation. Fill a box with books you no longer read. Donate the books to your church's library, a local library, or a thrift shop near you so others can enjoy them.

A delightful place. Describe your favorite place to read and what makes it so special.

Thankful hearts. Cover the tea table with a paper tablecloth. Decorate the tablecloth with simple heart-shaped drawings. (Or cover the table with a sheet of wrapping paper that has a heart design.) During the tea party, write one thing you're thankful for on each heart.

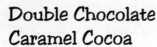

Menu Suggestions

Have fun in the kitchen as you work together to create these teatime treats!

Double Chocolate Caramel Cocoa

Ingredients

2 packets of hot chocolate mix

20 chocolate chips

2 teaspoons of caramel flavored ice cream topping or caramel dip

20 mini marshmallows

Directions

1. Fill two mugs with hot water or milk, as directed on the hot chocolate packets.
2. Pour in the contents of each packet and stir well.
3. Add 10 chocolate chips and one teaspoon of caramel topping to each mug and stir.
4. Top with 10 mini marshmallows.
5. Enjoy your warm drinks as you talk about being content.

Mini Book Sandwiches

Ingredients

four slices of sandwich bread
thin slices of meats and cheeses
condiments
one carrot

Directions

1. Cut the crusts off the slices of sandwich bread.
2. Lay several slices of meat and cheese on two slices of bread.
3. Add condiments, top with another piece of bread, and then cut the square sandwiches into two or four book-shaped rectangles each. (The bread represents book covers and the meat and cheese represent pages.)
4. Use a carrot peeler to peel the carrot. Shave off four 5-inch long strips from the carrot. Insert a long shaving of carrot between the pages of each book to represent a bright bookmark.
5. Enjoy your mini book sandwiches while you sip your hot drink.

Pretzel Party Pops

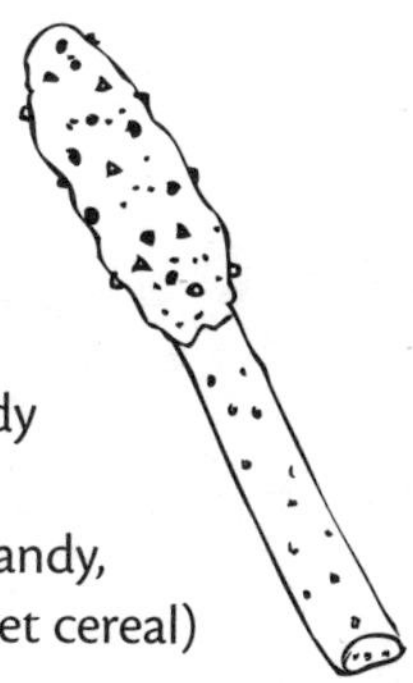

Ingredients

chocolate or white chocolate candy coating (for melting)
baking sprinkles (small pieces of candy, chopped nuts, dried fruits, sweet cereal)
waxed paper
pretzel rods

Directions

1. Slowly melt the chocolate in a microwave or in a double boiler on the stovetop.
2. Spread the chopped candies, nuts, and/or fruit on a sheet of waxed paper.
3. Dip a pretzel rod in the melted chocolate, about halfway up the rod.
4. Sprinkle the baking sprinkles or other small edibles over the chocolate-dipped end of each pretzel and place on waxed paper.
5. Let cool and enjoy.

Mom and Me

Chapter 4

Kindness Counts

We are God's workmanship, created in Christ Jesus to do good works, which God prepared in advance for us to do.

EPHESIANS 2:10

How do you feel when someone shows kindness to you? It's wonderful, isn't it? God has been kind and good to you, and He wants you to do the same to others. God wants you to treat people the way you would like to be treated. This is sometimes referred to as "the golden rule." God's Book has a lot to say about being kind and doing good things for others. The Bible speaks of doing "good works" for believers and unbelievers. That means forgiving people, being helpful, and doing nice things for other people. It often means helping others before you do something for yourself. God wants you to show kindness by letting others go first in line, offering them the biggest slices of pizza, and allowing them to choose what games you will play together.

If you have trouble thinking of good things to do for others, don't worry! God has planned lots of good works and kind acts for you to do. All you have to do is look for and notice opportunities He will give you. You can look for girls who may not have many friends and show them kindness. You can say kind things to people so they will feel appreciated. Encourage people by offering to help. Remember to be generous.

Think of the difference you can make by showing kindness in your home, at school, at church, on your sports team, at other activities, and wherever you go. Remember, God wants you to love others because He loves you!

The Bible Says...

*Always try to be kind to each other
and to everyone else.*

1 THESSALONIANS 5:15

Think about this verse as you work through the lesson.

Memorize It!

See who can be the first to memorize this verse.
Once you have it in your heart, check it off.

Mom ☐

Me ☐

Sharing Our Thoughts

Make my joy complete by being like-minded, having the same love, being one in spirit and purpose.

PHILIPPIANS 2:2

Talk about these questions and ideas together. Write down some of your thoughts in the spaces provided.

1. What are some ways you can be kind to the members of your family?

2. Tell about a person in your life who has shown kindness to you.

3. Share about a "good work" you have done for someone.

4. Tell about someone you know who is often kind. Do you enjoy being around this person? How does he or she make others feel?

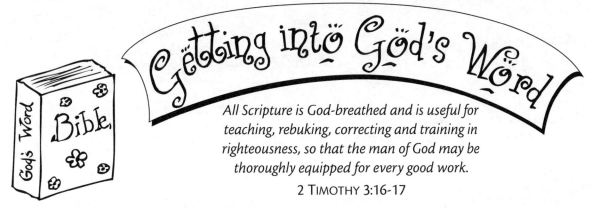

Getting into God's Word

All Scripture is God-breathed and is useful for teaching, rebuking, correcting and training in righteousness, so that the man of God may be thoroughly equipped for every good work.

2 TIMOTHY 3:16-17

Open your Bibles to Acts 16:13-15. After Jesus died, the number of believers grew rapidly. The apostle Paul and his companions traveled and spread the Good News of Jesus Christ throughout the region and beyond. Back then, Paul and the apostles preached outdoors or in people's homes. They didn't have church buildings where they would meet at nine o'clock every Sunday. In Acts 16:13-15, we meet a woman named Lydia who became a believer in Jesus. She invited Paul and his fellow travelers to stay in her home. She probably gave them food to eat, a place to sleep, and helped meet their needs in other ways as well. Lydia showed kindness to others because of her love for the Lord.

Read Acts 16:13-15 aloud together. Talk about how Lydia showed kindness to Paul.

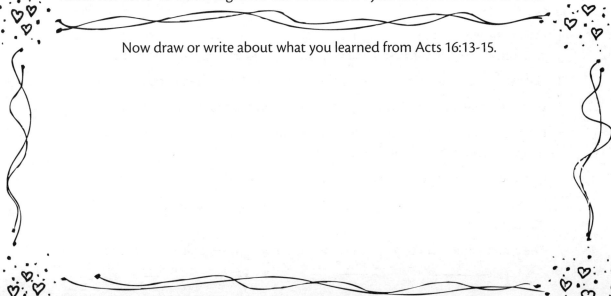

Now draw or write about what you learned from Acts 16:13-15.

Having Fun Together

Kindness Counts Weekly Calendar

Here's What You Need

- ✩ black marker
- ✩ two 3 x 11 strips of white paper
- ✩ two 8½ x 11 (or larger) sheets of colored, heavy-duty paper
- ✩ glue stick
- ✩ Crayons, colorful markers, colorful scraps of paper, sequins, glitter, foam art shapes, beads, buttons, colored pipe cleaners, colorful pompons, and so forth
- ✩ *Optional:* photos of family, friends, and you

Here's What to Do

1. Divide the white stripes into 7 equal sections as shown. Label each section at the top with one day of the week, starting with Sunday and ending with Saturday.
2. Glue the white calendar strip along the bottom of the colored paper.
3. Write "Kindness Counts!" in fancy lettering across the top of the calendar.
4. Be creative and decorate the calendar using your art supplies. You can also add photos of your family, your friends, and you if you'd like.
5. Record the good deeds and kind acts you do on each day of this special calendar.
6. Have fun comparing calendars and talking about how you practiced kindness throughout the week.
7. Add a new white strip to your calendars and repeat this activity next week.

Just God and Me

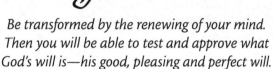

Be transformed by the renewing of your mind.
Then you will be able to test and approve what
God's will is—his good, pleasing and perfect will.

ROMANS 12:2

Look up these Scripture passages during the week to help you discover more about being kind.

Day of the Week	Verse	Something to Think About
Monday	Matthew 5:14-16	When others see your good deeds what will they think about you?
Tuesday	Romans 12:10	How can you honor someone in your family above yourself?
Wednesday	Ephesians 2:10	What are some of the good works God has prepared for you to do?
Thursday	Galatians 6:10	Think of people in your church you can help. Make a list of good works and then carry them out.
Friday	Ephesians 4:32	Jesus showed kindness by forgiving you. As an act of kindness, is there someone you need to forgive?
Saturday	Romans 12:13	What are some things you can share with others?
Sunday	1 Thessalonians 5:15	Has someone been unkind to you? How can you show him or her kindness back?

Talking to God

Devote yourselves to prayer, being watchful and thankful.
COLOSSIANS 4:2

Pray this prayer or write your own prayer thanking God for His kindness to you. Ask Him to help you become a kind person with a life filled with good works.

Dear God,
Thank You so much for showing kindness to me. And thank You for sending Your Son, Jesus, to pay for my sins. I'm so thankful for all the good things You've done for me. Help me become more like You. Please remind me to be kind to others. Show me ways I can help. I want my life to be filled with good works and kind acts so people will see You in me.
In Jesus' name I pray. Amen.

Things to Pray About

Think of one thing each of you needs prayer for. Write them down in the space provided. Talk about them together, and remember to pray for each other this week.

Daughter

Mom

Do not be anxious about anything, but in everything, by prayer and petition, with thanksgiving, present your requests to God.
PHILIPPIANS 4:6

Proverbs 31 for Girls

The Proverbs 31 girl looks for opportunities to show kindness to the people around her.

Many women do noble things, but you surpass them all.

PROVERBS 31:29

After reading Proverbs 31:29, think about what you can do to become more like the woman in Proverbs 31.

My Plan

1.

2.

3.

A Mother's Insight

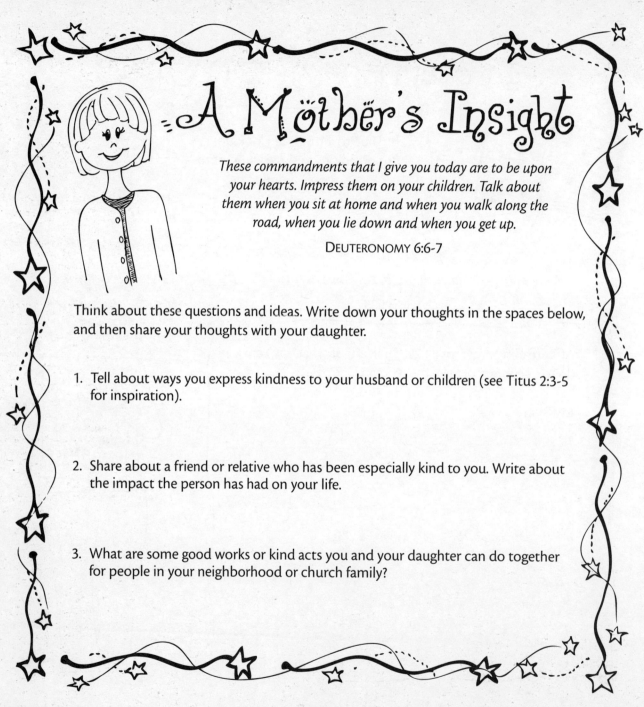

These commandments that I give you today are to be upon your hearts. Impress them on your children. Talk about them when you sit at home and when you walk along the road, when you lie down and when you get up.

DEUTERONOMY 6:6-7

Think about these questions and ideas. Write down your thoughts in the spaces below, and then share your thoughts with your daughter.

1. Tell about ways you express kindness to your husband or children (see Titus 2:3-5 for inspiration).

2. Share about a friend or relative who has been especially kind to you. Write about the impact the person has had on your life.

3. What are some good works or kind acts you and your daughter can do together for people in your neighborhood or church family?

Great Games Tea Party

Whatever you do, whether in word or deed, do it all in the name of the Lord Jesus, giving thanks to God the Father through him.

COLOSSIANS 3:17

Creating a Fabulous Tea Party Setting

Along with the party supplies and suggestions in the Introduction, add some of these special touches:

- Create a decorative table runner by rolling a length of colorful sports/game-themed wrapping paper down the center of the tea table.
- Gather an assortment of sporting equipment your family enjoys and display the balls, gloves, skates, racquets, and mallets near the table. (Or set up your tea outdoors on a blanket, and place the equipment around the border of the blanket.)
- Display "team pictures" and other sports-related photos of your family and you. Be sure to include pictures of your mom and dad!
- Stack favorite family board games on or near the table.
- Gather sporting events memorabilia and display them about the table: game schedules, ticket stubs, programs, team pennants, team hats, team jerseys.
- Put on your tennis shoes and wear your favorite sports outfit!

Tea Party Psalm

Read Psalm 145 aloud together. Talk about some of the ways God shows kindness to His people as stated in this psalm and how He shows kindness to you.

Having Fun Together

Kindness cards. Get 10 slips of paper or 3 x 5 note cards. Each person takes five cards, thinks of five people she knows, and writes the names down, one per card. Mix up the cards and stack them face down on the table. Take turns drawing a card, discuss what kindness that person would appreciate, and then follow through and do it.

Board game. Use tag board and art supplies to create a board game. You'll also need a number cube or die. Draw a wide, curvy path for your trail. Mark out spaces and add directions in some of the squares, such as "Move ahead one," "Move back two," "Say something kind," "Do something kind," and so forth. Create fun markers to use on the board.

Caught being kind. Write "I caught you being kind!" on a small piece of card stock. Punch holes and use string to make a short necklace. Tie it on a favorite bean bag animal. Then be on the lookout for family members who are being kind. When you spot someone showing kindness, set the animal on the person's shoulder and say, "I caught you being kind!"

Kindness kick. Go outside and kick a soccer ball back and forth. Each time you kick the ball, say something encouraging and kind about the other person. Or you can toss a foam ball back and forth in your living room while exchanging kind words.

Poetry. Write a poem titled "Kindness Counts." Read your poems aloud to each other.

Exercise fun. Go for a walk, jog, or bike ride through your neighborhood. Discuss how you can show kindness to your neighbors, and then follow through during the week.

More Fun Ideas

Kindness counts squeeze ball. Fill a large balloon with flour. Squeeze out any air, and tie the balloon closed. Use a permanent marker and write "Kindness Counts!" on the squeeze ball. Add decorative designs. Let the ink dry. Have fun squeezing "the ball" as you think of ways to show kindness to others.

Pom-poms. Get some crepe paper in your favorite sports team's colors. Cut 12 eight-inch strips of the crepe paper for each pom-pom. Starting at one end, wind masking tape about 3 inches up the paper to form a handle. Watch a game together and cheer on your team or cheer on each other with encouraging words.

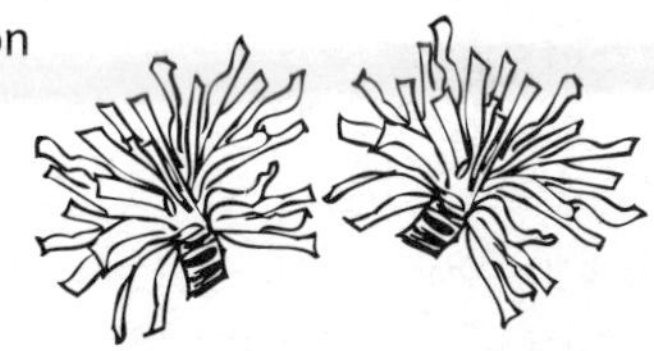

Team pennants. Cut a large piece of felt into a triangular pennant shape. Use art supplies to create a colorful pennant of your favorite sports team or athletic event.

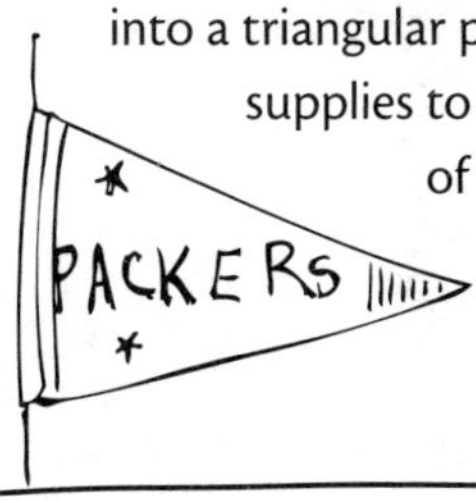

Family carnival. Create some homemade games (with prizes) for this special event, such as tossing rings onto soda bottles, throwing balls into a row of buckets, and tossing bean bags into a hoop or box. Be creative and have fun!

Obstacle course. Create a fun obstacle course in your backyard or living room. Use items from your garage and home to jump over, duck under, crawl through, and so forth. Gather the family and have each person run the obstacle course as quickly as possible. Use a stopwatch (or watch with a second hand) to note the time each person takes. Keep track of scores, and let everyone run the course twice, using the best of the two trials as that person's scores.

Menu Suggestions

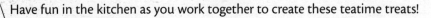

Have fun in the kitchen as you work together to create these teatime treats!

Team Colors Confetti Biscotti

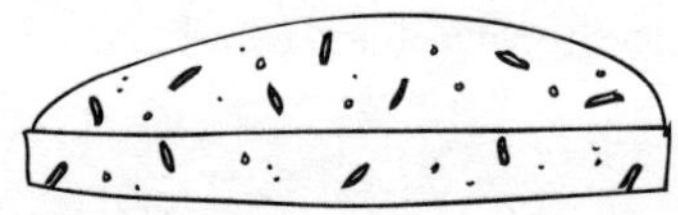

Ingredients

3 eggs
1 cup sugar
1 teaspoon vanilla
1 cup oil
3 cups flour
1 teaspoon baking powder
¼ cup colored sprinkles in your favorite sport team's colors
Optional: white chocolate, melted

Directions

1. Beat eggs, sugar, and vanilla thoroughly.
2. Stir in the oil.
3. In a separate bowl, combine the flour, baking powder, and sprinkles.
4. Add the dry ingredients to the wet ingredients and mix well.
5. Form the dough into three logs and place them on a greased cookie sheet. Flatten each log slightly into a 2 ½ x 9 loaf.
6. Bake at 350 degrees for approximately 25 minutes.
7. Cool for 10 minutes, and then cut into one-inch slices.
8. Place the cookies on their sides and bake them another 15 minutes or until lightly browned.
9. Let cool and enjoy.
10. *Optional:* Drizzle white chocolate over cooled cookies and top with sprinkles.

These crunchy treats travel well. Make a batch and take them to the next sporting event you attend.

Healthy Fruit Smoothie

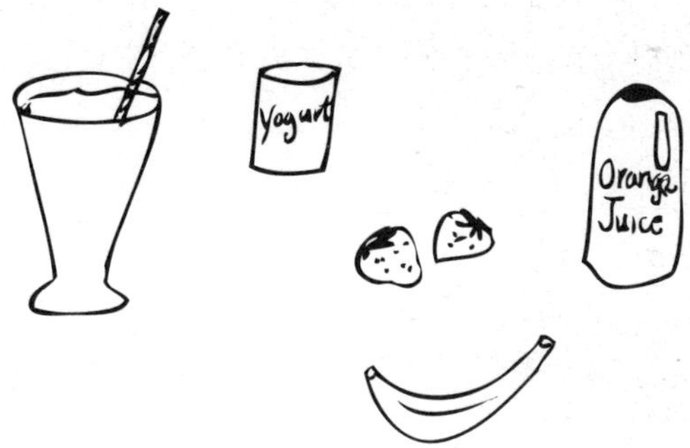

Ingredients

two 6- or 8-oz. containers of flavored yogurt
one banana
½ cup orange juice or other fruit juice
½ cup milk
8 ice cubes
6 fresh strawberries or 1 Tablespoon strawberry jam

Directions

1. Combine all ingredients in a blender and blend until smooth.
2. Enjoy this healthy beverage at your Great Games Tea Party.

Great Granola Bars

Ingredients

¼ cup light corn syrup
¼ cup brown sugar
1/3 cup peanut butter
5 regular marshmallows
1 teaspoon vanilla
2 cups crisp rice cereal

Optional

1/8 cup coconut
chopped nuts
½ cup chocolate chips

Directions

1. In a large saucepan, combine corn syrup and brown sugar.
2. Bring to a boil over medium heat, stirring constantly.
3. Remove from heat and stir in the peanut butter, marshmallows, and vanilla until combined.
4. Stir in rice cereal.
5. Add in optional ingredients if desired.
6. Press into a greased 9 x 13 pan. Let cool.
7. Cut and enjoy!

Milwaukee
Brewers

Mom and Me

Chapter 5

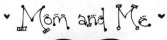

Friendship Matters

Love is patient, love is kind. It does not envy, it does not boast, it is not proud. It is not rude, it is not self-seeking, it is not easily angered, it keeps no record of wrongs. Love does not delight in evil but rejoices with the truth. It always protects, always trusts, always hopes, always perseveres.

1 Corinthians 13:4-7

Is one of your favorite activities spending time with your friends? Perhaps you even have a best friend you like being with the most. Friendship is one of the many good gifts God has given you. That's why God's Word has a lot to say about being a good friend…and about choosing your friends wisely.

The Bible says to honor your friends above yourself. What does that look like? It could mean letting your friend go ahead of you in the lunch line, letting her choose what song to play, or listening attentively when she tells a story.

Proverbs 13:20 says, "He who walks with the wise grows wise, but a companion of fools suffers harm." God wants you to choose friends who will be good for you—girls who are "wise" and will help you grow spiritually and obey God's Word.

God's Word also says that a friend should love at all times. That means even when your friend sins or acts in a way that isn't pleasing to God or others, you are to love her and forgive her.

Have you read Proverbs 27:17 before? "As iron sharpens iron, so one man sharpens another." This verse refers to friends helping friends become more like Christ and sinning less and less. God wants you to be a true friend by loving your friends enough to help them live His way. Maybe a friend of yours doesn't use the best language or doesn't treat others well. Perhaps you have a friend who disrespects her parents or gossips about other girls. God's Book says you get to help "sharpen" her, help her live her life to please God.

Friendship is a wonderful gift from God, but it also takes some hard work and good thinking. Be sure to spend time studying God's Word so you know what it means to be a true friend and please God.

The Bible Says...

A friend loves at all times.

PROVERBS 17:17

Think about this verse as you work through the lesson.

Memorize It!

See who can be the first to memorize this verse.
Once you have it in your heart, check it off.

Mom ☐

Me ☐

Sharing Our Thoughts

Make my joy complete by being like-minded, having the same love, being one in spirit and purpose.

PHILIPPIANS 2:2

Talk about these questions and ideas together. Write down some of your thoughts in the spaces provided.

1. What are some activities you enjoy doing with your friends?

2. Name one specific friend and share how you two are alike and different.

3. Do you and your closest friends believe the same things about God, such as who He is and how to live for Him? Explain.

4. What are some things you can do to be a good friend to others?

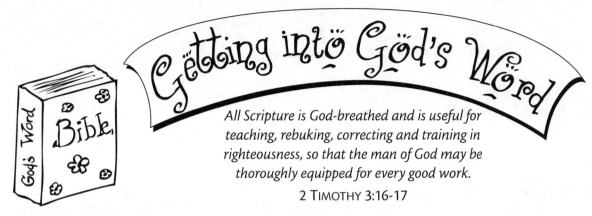

Getting into God's Word

All Scripture is God-breathed and is useful for teaching, rebuking, correcting and training in righteousness, so that the man of God may be thoroughly equipped for every good work.

2 TIMOTHY 3:16-17

Open your Bibles to 1 John 4:7-12. In this passage, John is writing to a group of people who believe in Jesus. He wants the people of God to show their love for Him by loving each other. John explains that God showed His love for us by sending His Son Jesus to die for our sins. That way we can live forever in heaven with Him. John writes that if we truly love God, we will show it by loving others.

Read 1 John 4:7-12 aloud together. Talk about ways you can show love to your friends so God's love will overflow from you to them.

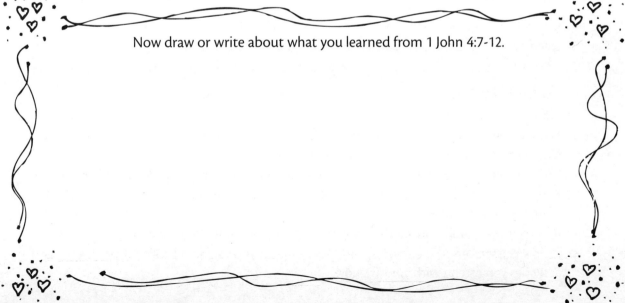

Now draw or write about what you learned from 1 John 4:7-12.

Having Fun Together

Friendship Treasure Box

Here's What You Need

- felt-tip marker
- construction paper, various colors
- sturdy box with a lid (a small shoe box would be perfect)
- collage materials: ribbon, buttons, dry pasta, dry beans, sequins, beads, stickers, felt, fabric scraps, seashells, photos of friends, and so forth
- glue gun and glue

Here's What to Do

1. Write the names of your good friends on the colored construction paper. Use fun and fancy lettering.
2. Cut out each name and glue it to the outside of the box.
3. Decorate the box using the collage materials, making it special and unique.
4. When the box is finished, display it on your dresser or in a special place.

Using Your Friendship Treasure Box

- Store photos of your friends.
- Write down Scripture verses from this chapter on pretty cards and store them in the box. Display a different verse each week and memorize it.
- Write down the prayer requests of your friends and what you know they could use help on. Keep them in the box, taking them out to pray about them. Leave space on the cards to write down God's answers!
- Keep stationery and note cards in the box. Use them to encourage friends.
- Keep small souvenirs, mementos, and other objects you value and collect from events and activities you attend with your friends.

Just God and Me

Be transformed by the renewing of your mind.
Then you will be able to test and approve what God's
will is—his good, pleasing and perfect will.

ROMANS 12:2

Look up these Scripture verses during the week to help you think like God does regarding friendship.

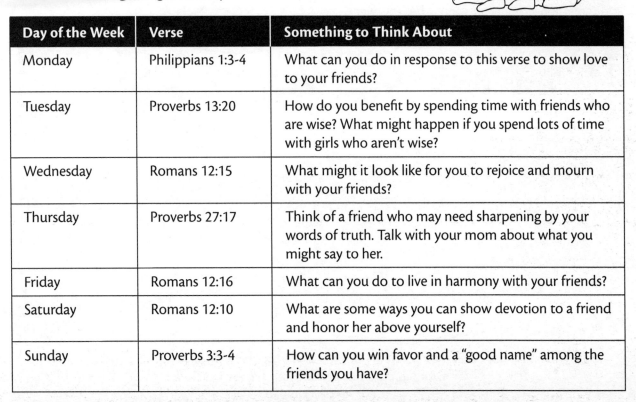

Day of the Week	Verse	Something to Think About
Monday	Philippians 1:3-4	What can you do in response to this verse to show love to your friends?
Tuesday	Proverbs 13:20	How do you benefit by spending time with friends who are wise? What might happen if you spend lots of time with girls who aren't wise?
Wednesday	Romans 12:15	What might it look like for you to rejoice and mourn with your friends?
Thursday	Proverbs 27:17	Think of a friend who may need sharpening by your words of truth. Talk with your mom about what you might say to her.
Friday	Romans 12:16	What can you do to live in harmony with your friends?
Saturday	Romans 12:10	What are some ways you can show devotion to a friend and honor her above yourself?
Sunday	Proverbs 3:3-4	How can you win favor and a "good name" among the friends you have?

Talking to God

Devote yourselves to prayer, being watchful and thankful.
COLOSSIANS 4:2

Pray this prayer or write your own prayer asking God to help you become a good friend to others. Thank Him for the friends He's already given you.

Dear heavenly Father,
Thank You so much for the gift of friendship. Help me put into practice what I've learned about being a good friend. Guide me as I show love for others as You command me to do in Your Word. I want to put others first and help them become more pleasing to You. Thank You for Your Word that teaches me how to be wise when I choose my friends. Your love is so great! Let my love for others be great because of You.
In Jesus' name. Amen.

Things to Pray About

Think of one thing each of you needs prayer for. Write them down in the space provided. Talk about them together, and remember to pray for each other this week.

Daughter

Mom

Do not be anxious about anything, but in everything, by prayer and petition, with thanksgiving, present your requests to God.
PHILIPPIANS 4:6

Proverbs 31 for Girls

The Proverbs 31 girl
works hard to be a good
and faithful friend.

Who can find a virtuous woman? for her price is far above rubies.

PROVERBS 31:10 KJV

After reading Proverbs 31:10, think about what you can do to become more like the woman in Proverbs 31.

My Plan

1.

2.

3.

A Mother's Insight

These commandments that I give you today are to be upon your hearts. Impress them on your children. Talk about them when you sit at home and when you walk along the road, when you lie down and when you get up.

DEUTERONOMY 6:6-7

Think about these questions and ideas. Write down your thoughts in the spaces provided, and then share your thoughts with your daughter.

1. Name one of your closest friends and share what you appreciate about her.

2. Tell about a specific time when a friend was kind or helpful to you.

3. Has a friend ever hurt you or sinned against you? How did you respond?

4. How can you do better at "sharpening" a friend to help her grow to become more like Christ?

5. Talk about a time when a true friend brought an area of sin to your attention because she wanted to help you become more like Christ.

Friendship Tea Party

Whatever you do, whether in word or deed, do it all in the name of the Lord Jesus, giving thanks to God the Father through him.

COLOSSIANS 3:17

Creating a Fabulous Tea Party Setting

Along with the party supplies and suggestions in the introduction, you can add some of these special touches:

- Invite another mother and daughter to your friendship tea party. Share with them what you've learned about being a good friend. Thank them for their friendship.
- Cover the table with white paper, and use colored markers to write your friends' names randomly on the tablecloth. Use fancy lettering.
- Cut an assortment of flower and heart shapes from colored paper. Write ways you can show love to a friend on each paper. Sprinkle them randomly on the table.
- Write some of the verses from this chapter on card stock. Use your fanciest writing. Display the verses in the tea party area.
- Display photos of your friends.
- Have yearbooks and photo albums out. Leaf through them and talk about the friends you've had and the things you enjoyed doing together.

Tea Party Psalm

Read Psalm 133 aloud together. David speaks about three specific blessings from God: unity, the anointing of a king, and the dew on the ground that provides moisture for crops. Discuss how wonderful it feels when friends are in unity about God and His Word.

Having Fun Together

Your friend Jesus. Read Proverbs 18:24. Talk about your friend Jesus and how He has made a difference in your life.

Reaching out. Talk about someone who may not have many friends. Brainstorm ways you could reach out to this person.

Friendship picnic. Plan a picnic. Write down your ideas for food, games, and activities. Decide who you will invite, set the date, send out invitations, fix the food, and celebrate the gift of friendship.

Art time. Draw pictures of your friends. Have fun as you try to identify the other person's friends using only the pictures.

Friendship piñata. Create a piñata! Blow up a large balloon. Dip one-inch strips of newspaper into a paper mache mixture of one part flour, one part water. Completely cover the balloon with the strips, removing excess solution. Let dry. Paint the piñata or cover with small strips of colored tissue paper. Cut an opening in the side and fill the piñata with candy or small trinkets. Close the hole and tape it shut.

Invite your friends over. With your mom and dad's help, your friends and you can take turns trying to break open the piñata with a stick. After you get the prizes out, share with your friends what you've learned about friendship.

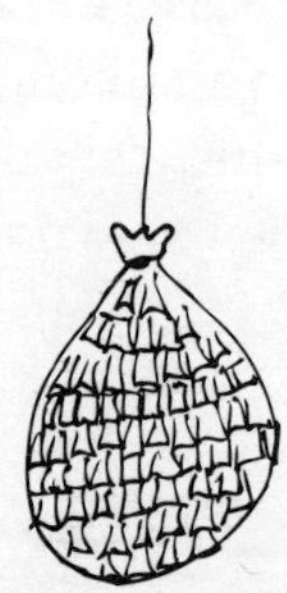

More Fun Ideas

A thank you. Write a note to a special person, thanking her for being a good friend to you.

Stick puppets. Use art supplies and craft sticks to create two puppets. Use the puppets to role play various situations involving the two "friends."

Helpful calendar. Working together, write the names of your friends on calendar pages, one name from each of you, per day. Each day pray together for the selected friends.

Word puzzle fun. Create a crossword puzzle or word search using the names of your friends. Exchange puzzles and have fun finding all the names.

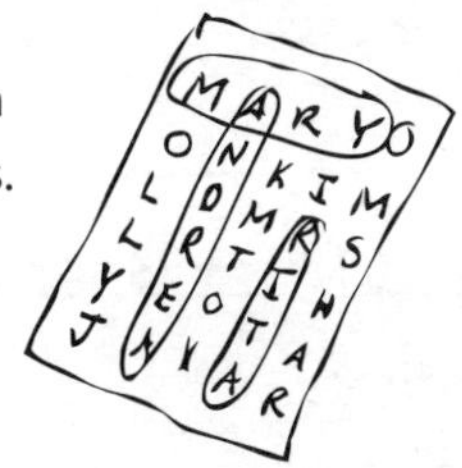

Friends on the fridge. Gather an assortment of pictures of your family's friends and display them on the refrigerator. At mealtime each day, take one photo to the table and pray as a family for that friend.

Menu Suggestions

Have fun in the kitchen as you work together to create these teatime treats!

Very Veggie Veggies and Dip

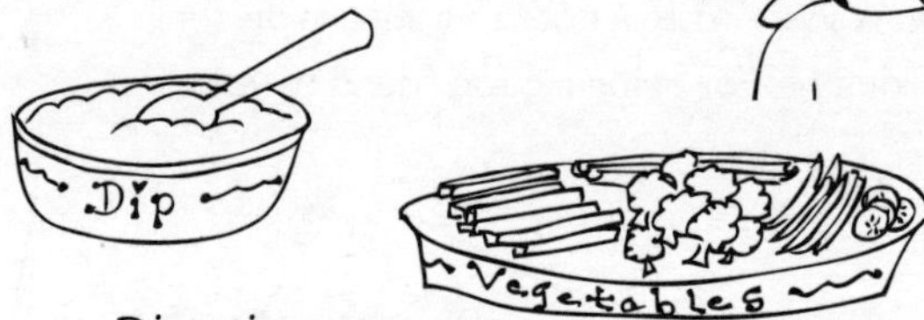

Ingredients

½ cup plain yogurt or sour cream
¼ cup mayonnaise
⅛ teaspoon each of garlic salt, seasoned salt, onion powder, dill weed
1 teaspoon minced onion flakes, chives
vegetables: your favorites, such as carrots, celery, cucumbers, green pepper, broccoli, cauliflower

Directions

1. Combine everything but the vegetables in a bowl. Stir well and chill.
2. Wash and cut the vegetables into small pieces.
3. Arrange the pieces in a colorful display on a special plate, along with the bowl of dip and a spoon.
4. Enjoy this healthy, tasty treat!

Fancy Root Beer Floats

Ingredients

vanilla ice cream
one can of root beer
chocolate sprinkles

Directions

1. Place two scoops of ice cream in each mug.
2. Pour half the root beer over the ice cream in each mug. Pour slowly as it will foam up.
3. Top with chocolate sprinkles.
4. Put a straw and a spoon in each cup.
5. Enjoy this sweet treat!

Sweet Cereal and Nut Trail Mix

Ingredients

1 cup each of three of your favorite cereals (bite-sized pieces work best)
assorted nuts
assorted dried fruit pieces

Directions

1. Combine the ingredients in a bowl and stir.
2. Pour the "trail mix" into a decorative bowl.
3. Munch on handfuls of the trail mix during your tea party.
4. For extra fun, pour the trail mix into cereal bowls, top with cold milk, and enjoy.

Chapter 6

Using God's Money

Since, then, you have been raised with Christ, set your hearts on things above, where Christ is seated at the right hand of God. Set your minds on things above, not on earthly things.

Colossians 3:1-2

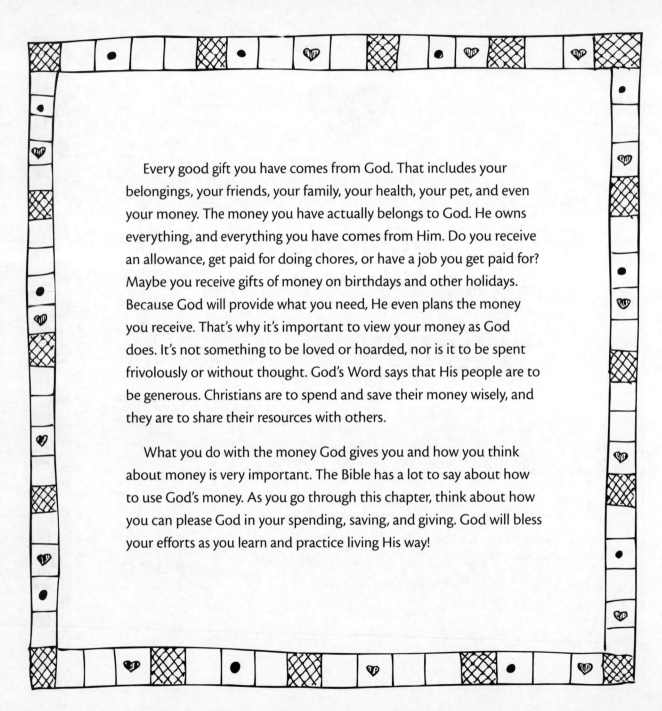

Every good gift you have comes from God. That includes your belongings, your friends, your family, your health, your pet, and even your money. The money you have actually belongs to God. He owns everything, and everything you have comes from Him. Do you receive an allowance, get paid for doing chores, or have a job you get paid for? Maybe you receive gifts of money on birthdays and other holidays. Because God will provide what you need, He even plans the money you receive. That's why it's important to view your money as God does. It's not something to be loved or hoarded, nor is it to be spent frivolously or without thought. God's Word says that His people are to be generous. Christians are to spend and save their money wisely, and they are to share their resources with others.

What you do with the money God gives you and how you think about money is very important. The Bible has a lot to say about how to use God's money. As you go through this chapter, think about how you can please God in your spending, saving, and giving. God will bless your efforts as you learn and practice living His way!

The Bible Says...

Be generous and willing to share.

1 TIMOTHY 6:18

Think about this verse as you work through the lesson.

Memorize It!

See who can be the first to memorize this verse.
Once you have it in your heart, check it off.

Sharing Our Thoughts

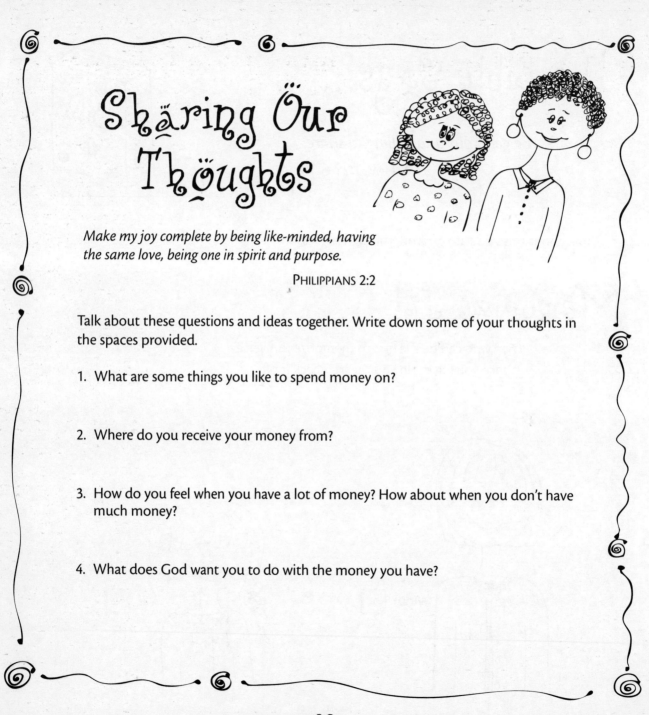

Make my joy complete by being like-minded, having the same love, being one in spirit and purpose.

PHILIPPIANS 2:2

Talk about these questions and ideas together. Write down some of your thoughts in the spaces provided.

1. What are some things you like to spend money on?

2. Where do you receive your money from?

3. How do you feel when you have a lot of money? How about when you don't have much money?

4. What does God want you to do with the money you have?

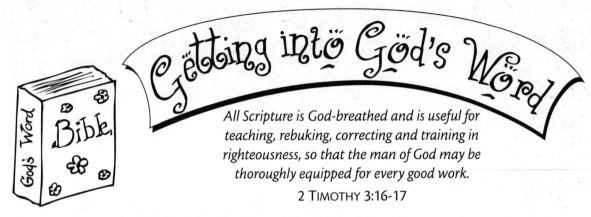

Getting into God's Word

All Scripture is God-breathed and is useful for teaching, rebuking, correcting and training in righteousness, so that the man of God may be thoroughly equipped for every good work.

2 TIMOTHY 3:16-17

Open your Bible to 1 Timothy 6:17-19. God's Word has a lot to say about money, spending, saving, and giving. It's a topic that's important to God. He wants you to enjoy what He gives you, but He also wants you to be generous, to do good, and to be wise with your resources. Some people think more highly of money than they ought to. These people can become greedy and selfish. Others are generous and quick to share what they have.

Read 1 Timothy 6:17-19 aloud together. Discuss how you can be rich through good deeds, generosity, and being willing to share.

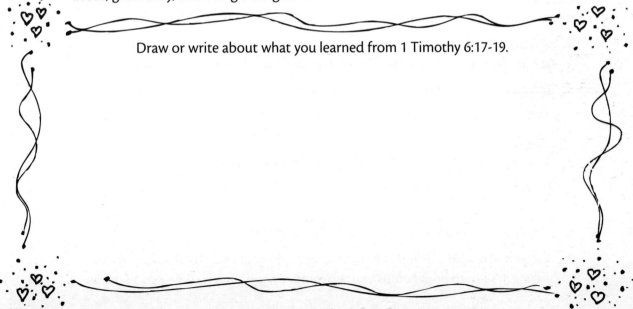

Draw or write about what you learned from 1 Timothy 6:17-19.

Having Fun Together

Fancy Purse

Here's What You Need

- ✩ 2 ten-inch strands of craft wire
- ✩ assorted beads
- ✩ colored card stock
- ✩ scissors
- ✩ colored markers
- ✩ transparent tape

Here's What to Do

1. Cut an eight-inch circle from the card stock and fold it in half.
2. Poke two holes on each side of the half circle near the top (for the handles).
3. Attach one wire to each hole by inserting it, bending a little bit of the end up to the wire on the other side of the hole and twisting.
4. String an assortment of beads onto each wire.
5. Insert the other end of each wire into the other hole and twist tie the ends to secure the two purse handles. Do your best to make both handles the same length.
6. Tape the sides of the purse together so your money won't fall through.
7. Use the markers and other art supplies to write "Use God's Money Wisely!" on one side of the purse. Write "Be Rich in Good Deeds!" on the other side.
8. Decorate the purse with creative patterns and designs.
9. Place some money inside this fun purse, and take it to church on Sunday for the offering. It's fun to be generous with your money and time by doing good deeds.

Just God and Me

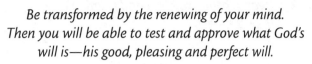

Be transformed by the renewing of your mind.
Then you will be able to test and approve what God's
will is—his good, pleasing and perfect will.

ROMANS 12:2

Look up these Scripture passages during the week to help you discover more about money and generosity.

Day of the Week	Verse	Something to Think About
Monday	Matthew 6:19-21	What are some things that you treasure? What good deeds can you do to store up more treasure in heaven?
Tuesday	Hebrews 13:5	What does God say about money and Himself in this verse?
Wednesday	Proverbs 8:10-11	What does God say is more important than silver, gold, and rubies?
Thursday	1 John 2:15-17	What things of the world are you tempted to love too much?
Friday	1 Timothy 6:9-10	What happens to people when they love money?
Saturday	James 1:17	How does this verse help you think about money?
Sunday	Proverbs 11:25	What does God say about being generous?

Talking to God

Devote yourselves to prayer, being watchful and thankful.
COLOSSIANS 4:2

Dear Lord,
I praise You for Your Word that teaches me how to think about money. Thank You for being generous and giving me so many good gifts to enjoy. Help me to use my money and my time in a way that will please You. Give me opportunities to be generous and do good deeds for others. I want to be wise, thankful, and content with the money and things You provide. In Your name I pray. Amen.

Pray this prayer or write your own prayer thanking God for His generosity to you. Ask Him to help you be generous and good to others.

Things to Pray About

Think of one thing each of you needs prayer for. Write them down in the space provided. Talk about them together, and remember to pray for each other this week.

Daughter

Mom

Do not be anxious about anything, but in everything, by prayer and petition, with thanksgiving, present your requests to God.
PHILIPPIANS 4:6

Proverbs 31 for Girls

The Proverbs 31 girl gladly shares what she has and is willing to help those in need.

She opens her arms to the poor and extends her hands to the needy.

PROVERBS 31:20

After reading Proverbs 31:20, think about what you can do to become more like the woman in Proverbs 31.

My Plan

1.

2.

3.

A Mother's Insight

These commandments that I give you today are to be upon your hearts. Impress them on your children. Talk about them when you sit at home and when you walk along the road, when you lie down and when you get up.

DEUTERONOMY 6:6-7

Think about these questions and ideas. Write down your thoughts in the spaces, and then share your thoughts with your daughter.

1. How were your parents examples to you in being generous with their time, money, and doing good deeds?

2. Tell about a time when you used your money to help somebody.

3. What are some ways you can be generous, give to others, and share what you have?

4. Share about a time when you spent your money foolishly.

Arts and Crafts Tea Party

Whatever you do, whether in word or deed, do it all in the name of the Lord Jesus, giving thanks to God the Father through him.

COLOSSIANS 3:17

Creating a Fabulous Tea Party Setting

Along with the party supplies and suggestions in the introduction, you can add some of these special touches:

- Display your art supplies at the table: paintbrushes, paints, modeling clay, crayons, markers, colorful paper, scissors, fabric, and so forth.
- Spend time together creating colorful designs and artwork. Display them in the tea party area.
- Make a poster that says "Arts and Crafts Tea Party." Put it on an easel by the door. Hang a paint-splattered apron or T-shirt near the easel.
- Gather artwork and craft items from your home and arrange them near the tea table. Include your own works of art!
- Check out arts and crafts books and magazines from your local library. Display them on the tea table.
- Use your fanciest handwriting to write "God is the great Creator! I can create things too!" on colored paper. Display prominently.

Tea Party Psalm

Read Psalm 62:1-12 aloud together. Talk about finding rest and contentment in God alone instead of trying to find them in things money can buy.

Having Fun Together

Needlecraft. Learn how to knit or crochet together. Have fun creating simple square dishcloths and coasters or scarves with colorful yarn.

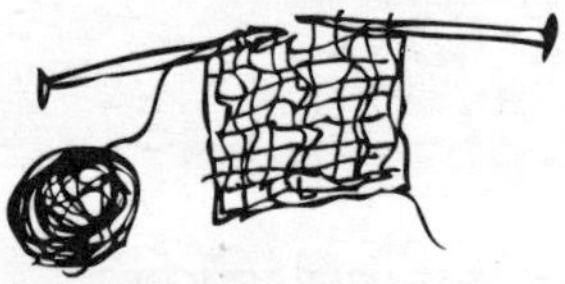

Fun with fashion. Use brightly colored embroidery floss to stitch several flower shapes on your favorite jeans. Use green fabric paint for the stem and leaves.

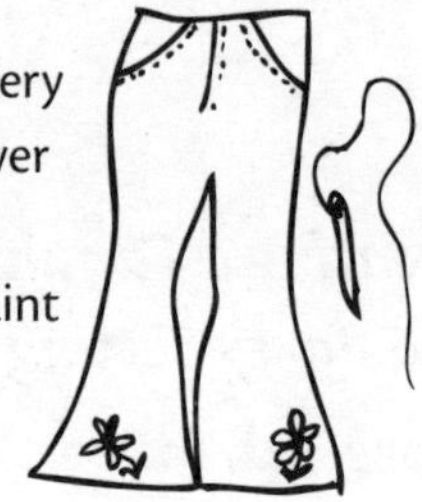

Something new. Try a new art medium such as charcoal drawing, wire sculpture, drawing with pastel chalks, wood crafts, modeling clay, or watercolors.

Art class. Plan and prepare to teach an art class to younger children. Invite one or two children from your church or neighborhood and teach them your favorite craft project.

Soap sculpture. Using four bars of inexpensive soap, carve a creative sculpture. Be very careful with the sharp knife! Display the sculptures in the bathroom or by the kitchen sink.

More Fun Ideas

Save and give. Tie a pretty ribbon around a clear glass jar. Print the words "Be generous!" on a decorative note card and attach it to the jar. Put the jar in a place convenient for the entire family. Have everyone add coins to the jar as the days and weeks go by. When the jar is full, take it to the bank and exchange it for dollar bills. Use the money to be generous to somebody else.

Art shirts. Use fabric paints to make your own fancy art shirt. Wear this "art smock" to protect your clothes while you create works of art.

Creative wrapping. Make your own wrapping paper! Cut open a brown bag, and then cut the bottom off. Dip common objects that will hold their shape when wet into shallow trays of paint. Press against the paper to make designs all over the paper. Let dry. Use the paper for the next generous gift you're going to give.

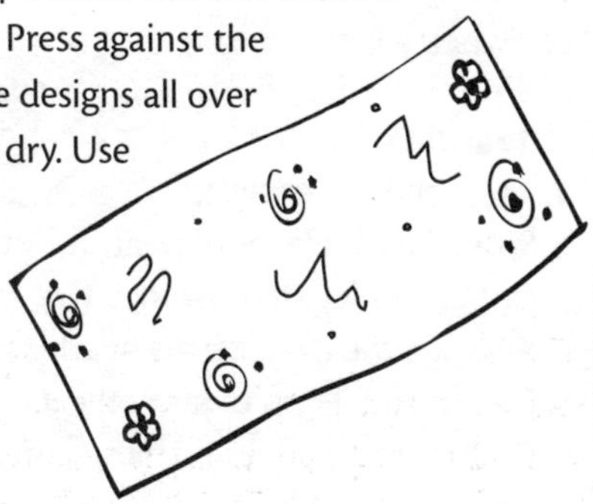

Wallets. Make decorative tri-fold wallets for your family. Cut an $8\frac{1}{2}$ x 11 sheet of paper or card stock down to 6 x $8\frac{1}{2}$. Fold this in half lengthwise. Tape the ends closed and then fold it into thirds. Write "Be generous" on each wallet. Add colorful designs. When you give these wallets to your family members, share what you've discovered about being generous.

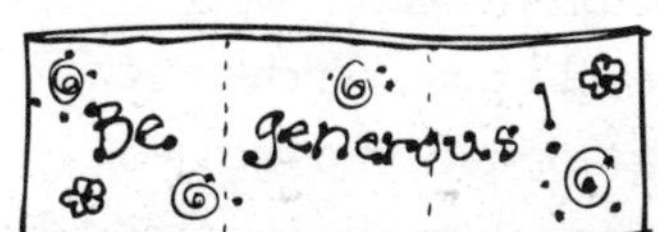

Menu Suggestions

Have fun in the kitchen as you work together to create these teatime treats!

Extra Special Ice Cream Drinks

Ingredients

ice cream (your favorite flavor)
1 banana cut into bite-sized pieces
½ cup chopped strawberries
½ cup milk
light whipped topping
chopped nuts
maraschino cherries
baking sprinkles, colorful

Directions

1. Combine the first four ingredients in a blender or mash the bananas and mix the ingredients together by hand.
2. Pour this creamy drink into two tall glasses.
3. Top with whipped cream, nuts, cherries, and baking sprinkles.
4. Insert straw and spoon…and enjoy!

Cream Cheese Roll-Ups

Ingredients

2 soft flour tortillas
cream cheese, softened
thin slices of ham or turkey

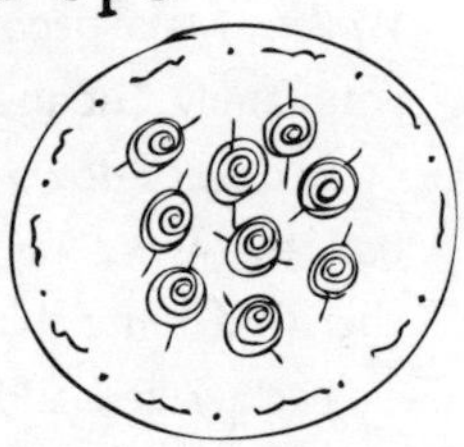

Directions

1. Spread cream cheese over each tortilla.
2. Top with a thin layer of ham or turkey.
3. Roll up tortilla tightly.
4. Cut the roll into half-inch slices.
5. Insert a toothpick into each roll.
6. Display on a decorative plate and enjoy.

Peanut Butter Toast Sticks with Jam

Ingredients

two slices of whole grain bread
peanut butter
strawberry jam

Directions

1. Toast the bread slices.
2. Spread a thin layer of peanut butter on each slice.
3. Cut each slice of toast into five thin "sticks."
4. Arrange the toast sticks neatly on each plate.
5. Place a small cup of jam on each plate.
6. Dip the toast sticks into the jam and enjoy during your Arts and Crafts Tea.

Mom and Me

Chapter 7

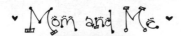

Home and Family—God's Perfect Plan

By wisdom a house is built, and through understanding it is established; through knowledge its rooms are filled with rare and beautiful treasures.

PROVERBS 24:3-4

God wants every girl to spend lots of time at home with her family. The Bible speaks often about the importance of the family and home. In fact, after God created the very first family—Adam and Eve—He "saw all that he had made, and it was very good" (Genesis 1:31).

Home is the special place where families can be together so parents can pass on the knowledge of God and His Word to their children. God then wants those children to grow up and do the same, passing His Truths along to the next generation so that more and more families are living to please Him. Your home and family are important to God, so they should be important to you as well.

Girls today spend a lot of time doing school activities, participating in sports, joining clubs, doing hobbies, and spending time with friends. These are all fine, but it's also very important you don't become overly busy with activities outside your home. Your relationships with your parents and your siblings are very valuable to God. He wants you to do well in them. Make your family and home your second priority (after God) in life so when you grow up you'll have all the talents and abilities you need to be a godly woman, wife, and mother.

The woman in Proverbs 31 is a good example of how women and girls can spend their time making the family and home top priorities. This woman did many special things to please God. She was blessed by God, and her children and husband praised her. You can look forward to many future blessings when you believe and practice what God's Word says about how important your family and home are.

The Bible Says...

Many women do noble things, but you surpass them all.

PROVERBS 31:29

Think about this verse as you work through the lesson.

Memorize It!

See who can be the first to memorize this verse.
Once you have it in your heart, check it off.

Mom ☐

Me ☐

Sharing Our Thoughts

Make my joy complete by being like-minded, having the same love, being one in spirit and purpose.

PHILIPPIANS 2:2

Talk about these questions and ideas together. Write down some of your thoughts in the spaces provided.

1. What activities do you enjoy with your family?

2. Name something that makes each person in your family special.

3. Share a favorite memory you have of your family being together.

4. What can you do to make your home an even better place to be?

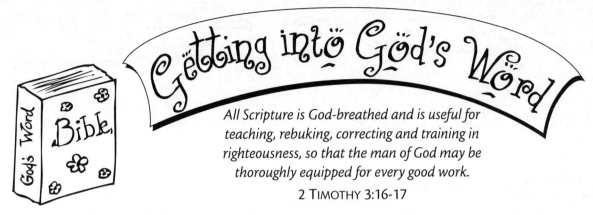

Getting into God's Word

All Scripture is God-breathed and is useful for teaching, rebuking, correcting and training in righteousness, so that the man of God may be thoroughly equipped for every good work.

2 TIMOTHY 3:16-17

Open your Bibles to Proverbs 31:10-31. The woman portrayed in Proverbs 31 is often looked to as the perfect example of being godly. As you read Proverbs 31:10-31, you'll find out about all the activities this woman does to help her husband and children. This woman loves God, and she shows it by making her family and her home top priorities.

Read Proverbs 31:10-31 aloud together to discover more about this hard-working woman who lives a joy-filled and faithful life before God and her family. After you read the passage, consider all the ways this woman served her husband and children and how God richly blessed her. Discuss how you can do the same.

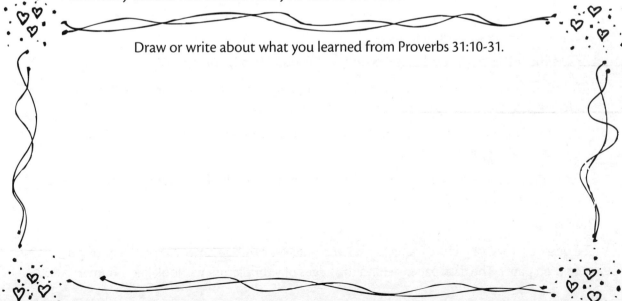

Draw or write about what you learned from Proverbs 31:10-31.

Having Fun Together

Framed Family Collage

Here's What You Need

- ☆ felt, fabric, or construction paper in various colors
- ☆ scissors
- ☆ glue
- ☆ picture frame, 8 x 10, with or without glass
- ☆ yarn, ribbon, and other art supplies
- ☆ card stock cut to fit inside picture frame

Here's What to Do

1. Using felt, fabric, or construction paper, cut out shapes of your house, your family members, and your pets. Add anything else you'd like to make the picture personal.
2. Glue the pieces to the card stock, creating a beautiful family collage.
3. Cut the yarn into short pieces and glue it to the page to add hair to each person in the picture. Use the art supplies to add other details to the scene.
4. Draw and cut out the letters to spell "Family First" (or write the words with marker) and glue them across the top of the page.
5. Place the completed project inside a picture frame and display it in your home to help you remember to put family and home first.

Helpful Tip

If you don't have a picture frame, center and glue your collage onto a larger sheet of dark-colored paper. The dark paper behind the edges of your picture will look like a frame.

Just God and Me

Be transformed by the renewing of your mind. Then you will be able to test and approve what God's will is—his good, pleasing and perfect will.

ROMANS 12:2

Look up these Scripture passages during the week to help you make your family and home top priorities.

Day of the Week	Verse	Something to Think About
Monday	Titus 2:3-5	According to these verses, what are some important things women and girls should be doing?
Tuesday	Proverbs 24:3-4	What special things can you get from God's Word to help you build a good home when you're older?
Wednesday	Romans 12:18	What are some things you can do to live "at peace" with your father, mother, and siblings?
Thursday	1 Timothy 5:14	If you marry and have children someday, what are some things you will do to "manage your home well"?
Friday	Proverbs 10:1	How can you bring joy to your father and mother?
Saturday	Deuteronomy 6:5-7	Why does God command parents to talk about His Word and His commandments with their children?
Sunday	Colossians 3:18-21	Talk about the specific commands God gives to each person in your family. How does His perfect plan help your family function well?

Talking to God

Devote yourselves to prayer, being watchful and thankful.
COLOSSIANS 4:2

Pray this prayer or write your own prayer praising God for creating His perfect plan for the family and home.

Dear Lord,
Thank You so much for creating the first family (Adam and Eve) and for giving me clear instructions on how to live within my family setting. Help me do well in making my family and home top priorities. I want to be alert so I can identify when I become too busy and forget that family and home are important. Thank You for being my heavenly Father and for loving me so much by giving me my family.
Amen.

Things to Pray About

Think of one thing each of you needs prayer for.
Write them down in the space provided. Talk about them together, and remember to pray for each other this week.

Daughter

Mom

Do not be anxious about anything, but in everything, by prayer and petition, with thanksgiving, present your requests to God.
PHILIPPIANS 4:6

Proverbs 31 for Girls

The Proverbs 31 girl works hard to be helpful around her home. She is of great value to her family.

She watches over the affairs of her household and does not eat the bread of idleness. Her children arise and call her blessed; her husband also, and he praises her .

PROVERBS 31:27-28

After reading Proverbs 31:27-28, think about what you can do to become more like the woman in Proverbs 31.

My Plan

1.

2.

3.

Bonus!

On the next page is a Proverbs 31 poster you can copy and put in your bedroom or school locker!

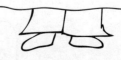

You Are a Proverbs 31 Girl!

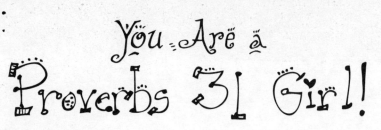

The Proverbs 31 girl...

- knows outward beauty lasts a short time but inner beauty pleases God and has everlasting value.
- is wise and faithful to God when she speaks.
- is strong in God's truth. She looks forward to the days ahead without fear because she knows there is a place prepared for her in heaven with her Lord.
- looks for opportunities to show kindness to the people around her.
- works hard to be a good and faithful friend.
- gladly shares what she has and is willing to help those in need.
- works hard to be helpful around her home. She is of great value to her family.
- lives her life to please her amazing God. And He greatly rewards her for her obedience to Him.

A Daughter's Reflection

Teach me to do your will, for you are my God; may your good Spirit lead me on level ground.

Psalm 143:10

Think about these questions and ideas. Write down your thoughts in the spaces provided, and then share your thoughts with your mom.

1. What are some ways you can spend your time at home more wisely?

2. Write down what you can and will do to be more helpful at home.

3. Are you too busy? If so, what changes can you make so you have more time to enjoy being at home with your family?

4. What can you do to improve your relationships with your father, mother, brothers, and sisters?

5. What activities can you do now to prepare yourself for the future...when you have a home of your own and if you become a wife and mother?

Nature Tea Party

Whatever you do, whether in word or deed, do it all in the name of the Lord Jesus, giving thanks to God the Father through him.

COLOSSIANS 3:17

Creating a Fabulous Tea Party Setting

Along with the party supplies and suggestions in the Introduction, add some of these special touches:

- Gather several plants (real or artificial) from your home and place them around the tea party area to create an outdoor setting...or hold your tea party outside!
- Display an assortment of bean-bag animals and insects among the plants.
- Put a beautiful bouquet of flowers on the tea party table.
- Collect items from nature, such as leaves, pretty rocks, seeds, seed pods, pine cones, leafy twigs, and flowers, and scatter them around the tea party area.
- Cut out pictures of God's beautiful creation from nature magazines. Post them around the tea party area.
- Take photographs of plants and animals you see near your home. Display the printed photos at the tea party table, and then put them into a photo album so you can enjoy them again and again.

Tea Party Proverbs

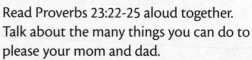

Read Proverbs 23:22-25 aloud together. Talk about the many things you can do to please your mom and dad.

Having Fun Together

Shadow box. Gather an assortment of interesting items from nature. Create a shadow box by setting a large box on its side. Arrange the objects inside to depict a beautiful scene from nature that highlights God's creativity. Use your art supplies to decorate and add details.

Decorative rocks. Gather a collection of smooth stones and use paints, markers, and other art supplies to decorate them.

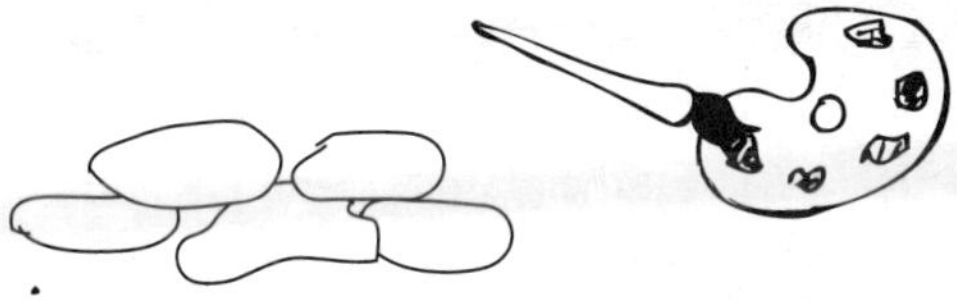

Sculptures. Collect an assortment of unique rocks and display them in a basket. Take turns creating rock sculptures using the collection.

Nature box. Cover a shoe box and lid (separately) with nature-themed wrapping paper. Use this treasure box to store your favorite nature finds.

Beautiful flowers. Create colorful tissue paper flowers! Stack three 8 x 10 or larger sheets of various colors of tissue paper. Fold the stack accordion style. Wrap one end of a chenille stick (or pipe cleaner) tightly around the center of the accordion-folded tissue paper so you have a stem. Carefully pull apart the pieces of tissue to create a puffy flower shape. Display several flowers in a vase at the tea party.

More Fun Ideas

Family celebration. Plan and prepare for a "We Love Family" celebration. Make decorations, fix special snacks, and place family photos and photo albums around the party area. Plan one or two activities, such as sharing how important family is, what people appreciate about their family members, and so forth. Invite your family at a selected time and date—and have fun!

A new look. Discuss how you can make the family living room more appealing and fun. Work together to rearrange the room and add some new, inexpensive touches, such as a wonderful bouquet of flowers or artwork family members have done. Have a favorite board game available so the family can spend time playing together.

Furniture art. Purchase an inexpensive piece of furniture from a thrift shop or garage sale. Work together to fix it up and paint it.

Compliment cards. Create "compliment cards" for the people in your family. Write several nice notes to each person (using copies of the stationery page at the back of this book). Both of you can sign them. Place the cards inconspicuously where the people will find them, such as in a lunch bag, under a pillow, or in a sock drawer.

Menu Suggestions

Have fun in the kitchen as you work together to create these teatime treats!

Fancy Chai Tea

Ingredients

hot water
2 tea bags of Chai tea, decaffeinated
cream or milk
sugar
cinnamon
nutmeg
light whipped cream topping

Directions

1. Bring a pot of hot water to boil.
2. Place a tea bag in each mug and fill the mugs with hot water.
3. Add a tablespoon of cream or milk, along with sugar to taste.
4. Top with a dash of cinnamon, a sprinkling of nutmeg, and a large dollop of whipped cream. Enjoy.

Tea Party Chips and Cheese

Ingredients

corn tortilla snack chips
salsa
shredded cheese

Optional

chopped tomatoes
green peppers
onions
black olives

Directions

1. Lay the corn tortilla chips on a microwave safe plate.
2. Pour salsa over the chips.
3. Sprinkle shredded cheese on top.
4. Add optional ingredients if desired.
5. Microwave for about 40 seconds or until the cheese begins to melt.
6. Cool slightly and enjoy.

Double Chocolate Chip Scones

Ingredients

2 cups flour

3 Tablespoons sugar

2 teaspoons baking powder

½ teaspoon baking soda

¼ teaspoon salt

½ cup butter, chilled

1 egg

½ cup milk

¼ cup semi-sweet chocolate chips

¼ cup white chocolate chips

Directions

1. Combine the first five dry ingredients in a bowl.
2. Cut in the butter and mix until the mixture is crumbly. Stir in the chocolate chips.
3. In another bowl, combine the egg with the milk.
4. Add the wet ingredients to the dry ingredients, and stir just until moistened.
5. Form into a ball. Knead the dough on a floured surface until almost smooth, about ten strokes.
6. Pat into a ¾-inch-thick circle. Cut the dough into 12 pieces and place on a greased cookie sheet.
7. Bake for 15-18 minutes at 375 degrees or until bottom of scone is lightly browned.
8. Let cool slightly, remove from pan, and enjoy.

Chapter 8

Knowing Our Awesome God

I will proclaim the name of the LORD. *Oh, praise the greatness of our God! He is the Rock, his works are perfect, and all his ways are just. A faithful God who does no wrong, upright and just is he.*

DEUTERONOMY 32:3-4

Think about the last time you received a gift that came with directions or an instruction manual, such as a new board game, an MP3 player, or a digital camera. Remember how you spent time reading the manual so you would learn about the gift and know how to use it?

God gave you His instruction manual too—the Bible—so you can get to know Him better and discover how to love Him by becoming more like Him. There is much to learn about our great God, and getting to know Him is an activity you will enjoy your entire life. As you read His Book, you'll learn that God is good, loving, gracious, merciful, perfect, holy, just, and righteous. You'll also learn about the gift of His Son, Jesus Christ, and God's perfect plan that enables you to spend eternity in heaven with Him.

To really know God and understand His thoughts, you'll want to spend lots of time with Him. Think about your busy schedule, and see what you can do to carve out pockets of time to spend in silence and solitude as you read God's Book and pray to Him. Turn off your music, the television, and the computer. Get away from all the noise and busyness of your life and be alone with God so you can think and talk with Him privately.

The more you know God, the better your life will be. He richly blesses those who seek Him, and He also gives His wisdom to those who ask for it. Make it a priority to be with God and learn to love His ways. As your relationship with Him grows stronger and deeper, you will find great joy in knowing your awesome Father in heaven and Jesus Christ, your Lord and Savior.

The Bible Says...

As for me, it is good to be near God. I have made the Sovereign LORD *my refuge; I will tell of all your deeds.*

PSALM 73:28

Think about this verse as you work through the lesson.

Memorize It!

See who can be the first to memorize this verse. Once you have it in your heart, check it off.

Mom ☐

Me ☐

Sharing Our Thoughts

Make my joy complete by being like-minded, having the same love, being one in spirit and purpose.

PHILIPPIANS 2:2

Talk about these questions and ideas together. Write down some of your thoughts in the spaces provided.

1. When do you most often think about God and His Word?

2. What can you do to have a closer relationship with Jesus and God?

3. Tell about your favorite place to pray or read your Bible.

4. Share what you know about God, Jesus Christ, and the Holy Spirit.

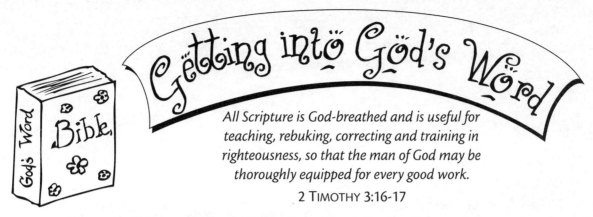

Getting into God's Word

All Scripture is God-breathed and is useful for teaching, rebuking, correcting and training in righteousness, so that the man of God may be thoroughly equipped for every good work.

2 TIMOTHY 3:16-17

Open your Bibles to Psalm 145. David, the author of many of the psalms, was the young man who slayed the giant Goliath and later became a great and famous king. David was also known as "a man after God's own heart" (1 Samuel 13:14). David wasn't perfect, but he knew God well and longed to please Him. He loved God very much. You can learn many things about God from David's words in Psalm 145.

Read this psalm aloud together so you can discover how you can know God better and become a "girl after God's own heart." Then talk about the amazing things that David wrote about our awesome God.

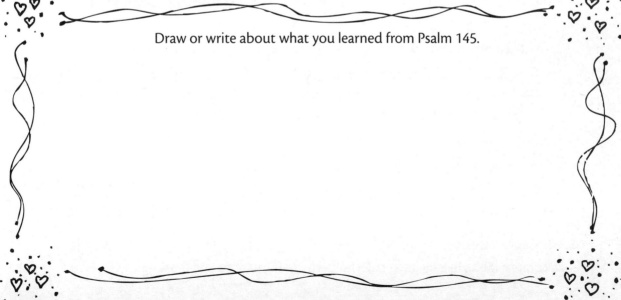

Draw or write about what you learned from Psalm 145.

Having Fun Together

Fabulous Bible Bag

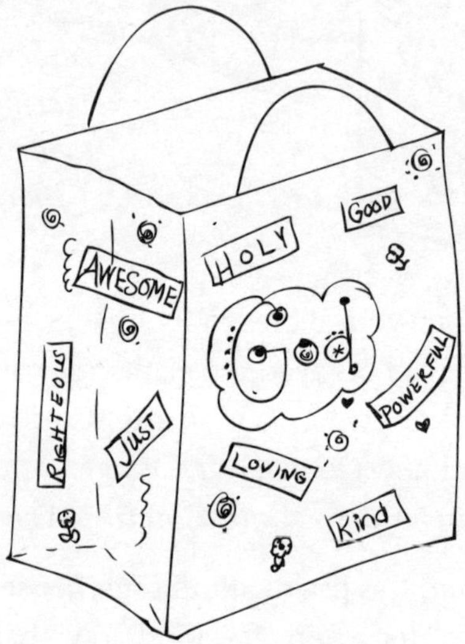

Here's What You Need

- ✩ sturdy paper "gift bag" with handles (a solid color works best)
- ✩ piece of corrugated cardboard
- ✩ ruler
- ✩ scissors
- ✩ glue
- ✩ colorful felt-tip markers
- ✩ magazines and newspapers

Here's What to Do

1. Measure the bottom of the bag and cut a piece of cardboard the same size. Put it inside the bag and glue it down to reinforce the bottom.
2. With a bright marker, write "God" on the front using your fanciest handwriting.
3. Think about words that describe God (such as "powerful," "wonderful," "amazing"). Search for words and cut them out of magazines and newspapers. For words you can't find, such as "righteous," cut out letters and spell them.
4. Glue the words artistically on the gift bag.
5. Add creative and fun designs using the colored markers.
6. What a great bag for carrying your Bible everywhere you go! You can read God's Word anytime...and share with others what you know about your awesome God!

Alternative Suggestion

Decorate a fabric bag by using colorful permanent markers and fabric paints.

Just God and Me

Be transformed by the renewing of your mind.
Then you will be able to test and approve what God's will is—his good, pleasing and perfect will.

ROMANS 12:2

Look up these Scripture passages during the week to help you get to know your awesome God better!

Day of the Week	Verse	Something to Think About
Monday	Psalm 46:10	Think of ways you can make time to "be still" so you can know God better.
Tuesday	Psalm 77:13-14	What do these verses say about God?
Wednesday	Psalm 62:11-12	What do these verses tell you about God? How do they help you live to please Him?
Thursday	1 Peter 5:6-7	How do these verses encourage you? How can you show humility before God?
Friday	1 John 5:14-15	What do these verses mean to you? How will you know what God's will is?
Saturday	John 17:1-4	What can you learn about God from Jesus' prayer in these verses?
Sunday	Hebrews 12:4-10	What do you think about God disciplining those He loves so they will grow in holiness?

Talking to God

Devote yourselves to prayer, being watchful and thankful.
COLOSSIANS 4:2

Dear God,
Thank You for being my heavenly Father. Thank You for being good, righteous, holy, and just. I love You for pouring out Your love and kindness in my life. You are a great God. Help me remember to spend time with You so I can get to know You and Your Son, Jesus Christ, better. Thank You, Jesus, for giving Your life so that I can be in heaven with You someday. I want to know You more and more each day so I will become more like You.
In Your name I pray. Amen.

Pray this prayer or write your own prayer praising God for who He is. Ask Him to help you know Him better.

Things to Pray About

Think of one thing each of you needs prayer for. Write them down in the space provided. Talk about them together, and remember to pray for each other this week.

Daughter

Mom

Do not be anxious about anything, but in everything, by prayer and petition, with thanksgiving, present your requests to God.
PHILIPPIANS 4:6

Proverbs 31 for Girls

The Proverbs 31 girl lives her life to please her amazing God. And He greatly rewards her for her obedience to Him.

A woman who fears the Lord is to be praised. Give her the reward she has earned, and let her works bring her praise at the city gate.

PROVERBS 31:30-31

After reading Proverbs 31:30-31, think about what you can do to become more like the woman in Proverbs 31.

My Plan

1.

2.

3.

A Daughter's Reflection

Teach me to do your will, for you are my God; may your good Spirit lead me on level ground.

PSALM 143:10

Think about these questions and ideas. Write down your thoughts in the spaces provided, and then share your thoughts with your mom.

1. List some of the ways God has shown His goodness to you.

2. What are some ways you can make more time to be with God and Jesus?

3. What have you learned about your awesome God in this chapter?

4. Write out a three-step (or more) action plan for getting to know God better.

Mom, Me, and Music Tea Party

Whatever you do, whether in word or deed, do it all in the name of the Lord Jesus, giving thanks to God the Father through him.

COLOSSIANS 3:17

Creating a Fabulous Tea Party Setting

Along with the party supplies and suggestions in the introduction, you can add some of these special touches:

- Cut music notes out of black paper and scatter them about the tea table.
- Create a festive poster that says "Mom, Me, and Music Tea Party" and place in the tea party area.
- Distribute CD cases of the music you both like throughout the tea room.
- Artistically display instruments, hymnals, and songbooks in the tea area.
- Play soft music as you enjoy your tea party and activities.
- In your fanciest handwriting, write these Scriptures on construction paper (folded so they stand up) or note cards and place them on the table.
  - "I will sing and make music to the LORD" (Psalm 27:6).
  - "The music of the strings makes you glad" (Psalm 45:8).
  - "Make music to him on the ten-stringed lyre" (Psalm 33:2).
  - "It is good to praise the LORD and make music to your name" (Psalm 92:1).

Tea Party Psalm

Read Psalm 111:1-10 aloud together. Talk about God's wonderful deeds listed in this psalm and some of the wonderful things He has done in your lives.

Having Fun Together

Music you like. Talk about your favorite Christian song. Explain how it helps you to know God more.

Become a songwriter. Write lyrics to a new song of praise to God.

O Lord,
You're an
amazing
God...

Doorknob sign. Make a fun doorknob sign like the one shown here. Get a 4 x 8 piece of craft foam or card stock. Cut a one-inch slit and a two-inch hole near the top. Write "Quiet please. I'm spending time with God" on the sign. Decorate it and hang it on your bedroom doorknob when you want alone time with God.

Quiet
please.
I'm
spending
time
with
God!

Make a maraca. Create a simple rhythm instrument to use when you sing favorite praise songs. Place 20 popcorn kernels or dry beans inside a plastic Easter egg and tape securely.

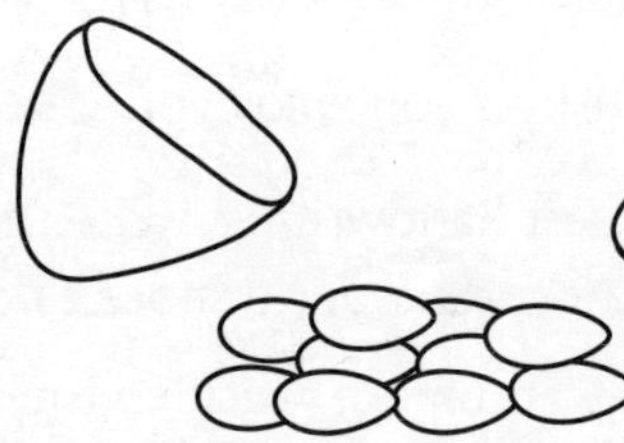

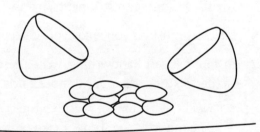

Praise box. Decorate a shoe box with art supplies. Write "Knowing God" on the outside in fancy lettering. Keep a stack of note cards near the box. Throughout the week, write down words or phrases that describe God and put them into the box. Also write about what God is doing in your life and place them in the box. At the end of the week, open the box together and read the note cards aloud. Praise God for His love and care.

More Fun Ideas

Sing a psalm. A psalm is a sacred song or poem used in worship. Try singing your favorite psalm. You can use a tune you already know or make up a new one.

A family band. Gather an assortment of rhythm instruments or household items that can be used as rhythm instruments. Play and sing your favorite praise song. Invite the entire family to join in.

A favorite hymn. Choose your family's favorite hymn (or pick one if your family doesn't have one) and sing it daily as you work together doing chores.

In the kitchen. Bake and frost a cake together. Use colorful icing to write words about God on the cake. Display the cake at your supper table. When you serve it for dessert, share what you're learning about getting to know God.

Menu Suggestions

Have fun in the kitchen as you work together to create these teatime treats!

Cherry Lemonade

Ingredients

Lemonade
maraschino cherries
  with cherry juice
one lemon

Directions

1. Pour two tall glasses of cold lemonade.
2. Add one tablespoon of the cherry juice to each glass and stir.
3. Poke toothpicks through three cherries. Drop one skewer of fruit into each glass.
4. Cut the fresh lemon into four wedges. Squeeze the juice from one lemon wedge into each glass. Place the remaining wedges in the glasses.
5. Stir and enjoy.

Our Own Snack Mix

Ingredients

mini crackers
small pretzels
cheese curls
popcorn
snack chips
peanuts or other nuts

Directions

1. Pour the assorted snacks into a large bowl and stir.
2. Serve in small, fancy bowls or colorful cupcake papers.

Perfect Party Pretzels

Ingredients

1 packet yeast (or 2¼ teaspoons)
1½ cups warm water (not hot)
1 Tablespoon + 1 teaspoon of sugar
1 teaspoon salt
4 cups of flour

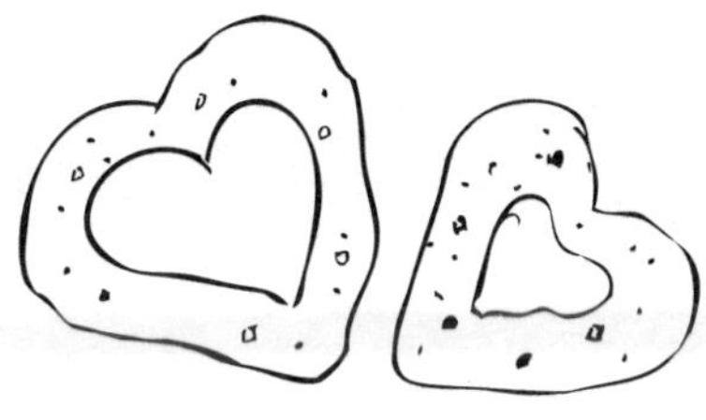

Optional

1 egg beaten
coarse salt
mustard
cheese, melted

Directions

1. Dissolve yeast in warm water for five minutes.*
2. Add the sugar and salt to the mixture.
3. Blend in the flour.
4. Knead dough until smooth, about seven minutes.
5. Cover and let rise until double in bulk (about one hour) and then punch down.
6. Cut dough into 12 pieces. Roll each piece into a rope about a half-inch in diameter.
7. Create heart shapes with the ropes of dough. Place on two greased cookie sheets.
8. *Optional:* brush with egg and top with coarse salt.
9. Bake at 425 degrees for 10 to 15 minutes until lightly browned.
10. Enjoy the heart-shaped pretzels as you talk about "having a heart for God."
11. For extra taste, drizzle mustard or melted cheese over the warm pretzels.

* *Note:* If you have a bread maker, place the ingredients in it and put it on the dough setting. When it's done, proceed to step 6.

"Mom and Me"